Pull-out Map of Penwith

West Cornwall in the Twentieth Century

LIFE IN PENWITH

Edited and Introduced by
Susan Hoyle

Written by
Ann Altree
Jenny Dearlove
Iris Green
Carlene Harry
Ron Hogg
Joan Howells
Susan Hoyle
Pam Lomax
Jean Nankervis
Tony Noonan
Margaret Perry
Glyn Richards
Dawn Walker

Published by Penwith Local History Group

First published in 2007 by
Penwith Local History Group
Morrab Library, Morrab Gardens
Penzance TR18 4DA

© Penwith Local History Group for the authors: Glyn
Richards, Ron Hogg, Carlene Harry, Joan Howells, Jean
Nankervis, Ann Altree, Dawn Walker, Susan Hoyle,
Jenny Dearlove, Iris Green, Pam Lomax, Tony Noonan
and Margaret Perry

ISBN 0-9540249-3-1

Designed by Pamela Lomax
Printed by Printout Printing Services Ltd, Threemilestone,
Truro

FRONT COVER IMAGE
Market Jew Street, Penzance c 1900
(Courtesy of the Morrab Library)

BACK COVER IMAGE
Market Jew Street, Penzance c 2000
(Courtesy Glyn Richards)

Contents

Acknowledgements

This book has been a collaboration between members of the Penwith Local History Group who would not have succeeded without the help and support of each other, and the continuing support of the Morrab Library.

More particularly:

Glyn Richards thanks David Chinn of Morrab Library, Penzance, for his information from the newspaper archive; Eddie Downing, former skipper and colleague, for his help corroborating material from their past service on the patrol vessels; the staff at the Cornwall Sea Fisheries Office, Penzance; and the crew of the Saint Piran.

Ron Hogg thanks Carlene Harry for providing information, photographs and family archive material; Joff Bullen for permitting the use of his photographs and for technical advice on the text; and the Cornish Studies Library for the use of their photograph.

Joan Howells would like to thank Mrs Trewey Curnow and Jane Howells.

Jean Nankervis thanks all those, both Zennor Codgers and others, who so generously gave their time and help.

Ann Altree thanks George and Simon De-Vey of Anderton & Rowlands for their help.

Dawn Walker thanks Jane Powning and Steve Hartgroves at the Historic Environment Service of Cornwall County Council, and also the archivists of Cornwall Record Office, the librarian at the Morrab Library, Penzance, and Mr J Holmes at Penlee House.

Susan Hoyle thanks Sue Griffin, who started her on this trail; Dr J Patrick Vaughan, Pip Benveniste, and Anne Crockett for their kindness in allowing her to tell the story of a small but vital part of their lives; William Hetherington (Hon Archivist, Peace Pledge Union); Josef Keith (Librarian, Library of the Religious Society of Friends in Britain) and John Makin; and Chris Coates, Pam Manasseh, Kate Perry, and the late Margery Ruhrmund.

Jenny Dearlove thanks members of the Cornwall Federation of Women's Institutes (CFWI) and office holders at Institute and County levels for their generous help; in particular the late Wilmay Le Grice, June Starnes, Mary Laity and other members of Madron WI; Jean Nankervis, Zennor WI; Iris Rowe, Gwinear Parish WI and Hayle WI, currently CFWI archivist.

Pam Lomax thanks Veronica Chesham, Gordon Bridger and Ashley Barker for their advice and encouragement.

Tony Noonan thanks church ministers and elders from twenty-one different faith groups, a total of thirty-two people. In addition, there was invaluable assistance from Diana Evans (Church of England Research and Statistics), Cedric Appleby (Methodist historian), and staff at both the Cornwall Centre and the Cornwall Records Office.

Introduction

Susan Hoyle

Mining's scat, fishing's scat, farming's scat: it's back to wrecking, me 'ansomes! (Cornish bumper sticker, c 2000)

West Cornwall in the Twentieth Century: Life in Penwith is a departure from the usual research of the Penwith Local History Group. While we might not go as far as Mao Tse-Tung, who (it is alleged) thought it too early to pronounce on the effects of the French Revolution, until now our published books have focussed on times well before we or our parents were born. However, any worries about the current focus on more recent events vanished as we read each others' drafts. While many of the great basic institutions, discoveries and inventions which underlie the quality of life in today's Britain began in the nineteenth century (e.g. free elementary education, public-health improvements, railways, the internal-combustion engine), their greatest impact came in the next century, and it is in tracing the influence of these and other changes on the ordinary people of Penwith that the deep interest of this book resides.

At the same time, one of the pleasures of editing a collection of articles on a common historical theme by different people, often with different interests and concerns, is finding links between the chapters. These overlaps help to emphasize how interconnected our lives are, and thus our history. Considering how small Penwith is in size and population—and for how many hundreds, even thousands, of years many of its families have been here—we should not perhaps be surprised at the continual coincidence of name and place and focus. Memories are long here, and meanings are complex. Because West Cornwall is such a well-defined and well-rooted place—a virtual island in fact as well as metaphorically— the connexions in its stories are more distinctive than they would be almost anywhere else in the country.

Our look at twentieth-century West Cornwall begins with Glyn Richards' patrol around the Penwith coast. We could not have a better guide than Glyn, whose roots here go deep: for example, his grandfather James Mann Hosking fished out of Newlyn in 1900 in a Mount's Bay lugger (a sailing vessel). For many years Glyn was a Fishery Officer and Engineer with the Cornwall Sea Fisheries patrol service, and thus knew the area in its heyday. When fishing was a major employer, he remembers the arrival in the 1970s and '80s of the large purse-seiners, from Scotland and the east coast during the Cornish winter mackerel season, their nets 'capable of encompassing St Paul's Cathedral' (p10). And by the time he retired in 2001, people were saying that fishing was 'scat'. (Perhaps it is, but today Newlyn lands the most valuable catch in the country, and in terms of weight is second only to Brixham.[1])

If on his first trip that cold day in January 1965, Glyn had looked up from tending the fenders and stowing the ropes of *Cornubia*, he would have glimpsed the roof of Wheal Betsy, high on the hill overlooking Newlyn. This was the house built by Thomas and Caroline Gotch in the Arts and Craft style in 1910 (and discussed in engrossing detail by Pam Lomax, in chapter 11). The Gotches' daughter Phyllis slept in her 'little white room' at Wheal Betsy for a few brief months before joining a vaudeville company in 1911 to tour South Africa. There she married the mining engineer Ernest Patrick Doherty and, like the women of the Harry family (to whom Carlene Harry introduces us in chapter 3), she came to understand the dangers of the mining life, where men worked underground in heat, cold and dust for hours at a time, often standing up to their knees in water. She saw it herself at Langlaagte mine, where she was 'the first woman who ever went down below the levels the skip goes down to...the 17th level and all through it'.[2] Charles Harry (see Ron Hogg's account of Charles' travels in chapter 2: Charles was Carlene's grandfather) had worked in this same mine when he was a migrant worker in South Africa. Unlike Ernest Doherty, who had trained at the Camborne School of Mines, he had learned his trade in the under-sea mines at Levant and Botallack. Both 'Erne' and 'Charlie' went to South Africa because of a recession in the Cornish mining industry, and they both contracted the miner's lung-disease phthisis, Doherty dying in 1918 and Harry in 1939.

---

[1] Monthly Return of Sea Fisheries Statistics.
[2] Phyllis Gotch to her parents, August 1911, Wheal Betsy Archive. This quotation is from Pam Lomax' forthcoming book on Phyllis Gotch.

Yet another link: Joan Howells (on Goldsithney School, chapter 4) mentions Father Bernard Walke's shocked reaction to the sudden death of mother-of-six Mrs Laity in the 1918 'flu epidemic; Tony Noonan reminds us (in chapter 12, on Christianity in twentieth-century Penwith) that the high Anglican Walke, while still vicar of St Hilary, was a national figure in the 1920s and '30s.

Or again: Zennor 'Old Codger' John Loosemore remarks (chapter 5) that in World War II 'no one lived in Carn Cottage...' This is the house where Gerald Vaughan (the benefactor of the pacifist farming group which Susan Hoyle writes about in chapter 8) lived with his wife Ellaline and later his son Patrick in 1937. It is up a rough track which begins opposite Eagle's Nest, spied by Glyn on his sea-cruise (chapter 1). John Loosemore remembers nothing of Gerald Vaughan's pacifist activities, but he does remember buying his car, a Morris 8 open tourer. John also knew John Crockett (another pacifist discussed in chapter 8): Crockett had an 'iron horse' (a motorized plough with two wheels, and two handles—you walked behind it) and he ploughed one of Loosemore's neighbour's fields with it.[3] Another couple of Jean's Old Codgers from chapter 5, Nora Jelbert and Arthur Mann, were married on 8 April 1950 in Pendeen Church, with a sit-down wedding reception for 100 guests to follow in St. John's Hall, Penzance. Chirgwin's did the catering—and their instructive history is the subject of Iris Green's chapter 10.

Our final chapter, Margaret Perry's informative and entertaining account of the coming of the motor-car to Penwith, not surprisingly has echoes throughout the book: for instance, John Loosemore (chapter 5) recalls that his father Ernest 'was brought up in London and was trained as an electrician.... Later he became a motor engineer and worked for Lord Cowdray as a chauffeur. By 1909 he had an international driving license with his picture on and all.' We recall how much changed with the arrival of the car when we read of Clifford Harry playing in the road at Carnyorth because there were never any cars about (chapter 3), or (as late as the 1940s) the pacifist farmers taking produce to Penzance in a pony and trap (chapter 8).

Iris Green's chapter (10) on the old Penzance-based grocery business of Chirgwin & Son is a case-study in the decline of the local shop. Chirgwin's once had shops all over this district, and here too (to pursue my links-theme) the car played a part—at St Ives:

> [t]he replacement of horse-drawn vehicles by motor-vans for deliveries required capital outlay. ... [T]he purchase of a Ford No 8 to replace the horse vehicle for deliveries was delayed when the Golf Club business was lost. In the early years of the twentieth century most people walked to Penzance from the various centres of population within West Penwith. From 1890 to 1920 the Royal Mail coach provided four regular services six days a week with an extra one on market days from St Just to Penzance. Motor-buses followed. The pony and trap for personal mobility was superseded by the motor-car.[4]

And now we drive beyond Hayle to queue at Marks & Spencer...

Dawn Walker's 'Groping in the Dark' (chapter 7)—about changing attitudes to archæology in what is arguably the richest archæological area in Britain—underlines the social significance of the motor-automobile, when she says that 'by the first World War, private cars...made life easier for those wanting to visit ancient monuments'—visits to view or, even more importantly, to dig. Excavations in Penwith at this period used new techniques to great effect, producing detailed reports, drawings and plans, and setting the standard for years to come.

The West Cornwall Field Club (founded in 1935 and expanded in 1982 as the Cornwall Archaeological Society [CAS]) would never have been the success it was without (amongst other things) the mobility the car gave to its members. From 50 at the Field Club's inception, by 1986 the CAS had 700 members.[5] This healthy state of affairs gave archæology clout with local government, and it is probably no coincidence that Cornwall County Council was amongst the first to appoint a full-time professional archæologist (within what is now called the Historic Environment Service), nor that the relationship with the CAS has been closer and more fruitful than in many other counties. It is relevant also that at the end of the century, CAS membership was down from that peak, at fewer than 600. We are no longer as apt as we were to use our greater mobility in collective endeavours.

---

[3] Information via Jean Nankervis.

[4] Below, p.86

[5] Cornish Archæology Society Website (editorial of its *Journal* 25 (1986)).

Three chapters centre on childhood. Carlene Harry (chapter 3) has used her father's notebooks to great effect to recreate what a boy-child's out-of-school life was like in the early years of the last century. Younger readers may find it hard to credit how much freedom those boys had! (Girls, of course, had much less liberty, and much more to do in the house.) Joan Howells (chapter 4) traces the history of the much-loved village school at Goldsithney. There are many names here which will bring a smile to anyone who knew Goldsithney then—for example, Miss Edmonds, headmistress 1930-55, and the school cleaner, Mrs Rowe. The other chapter (6) which touches closely on childish concerns is Ann Altree's study of the Corpus-Christi Fair, which for centuries must have been a highlight of a Penwith child's year—now a shadow, if a still glittering one, of its former self. Ann has relied greatly on the notes her grandfather, the renowned Penzance historian Walter Eva, made of his own childhood, and on her own memories of this annual treat.[6]

Not only did children's lives change—everyone's did. Jenny Dearlove's chapter (9) is an absorbing account of the Madron WI and the difference it made to the lives of so many women in this rural area. The changing rôle of women was one of the most vivid aspects of the last century—a revolution in educational, political and economic opportunities—and Jenny demonstrates how much, in its understated way, the WI was central to that revolution. And the WI also provides another path through our book: St Just WI are the authors of the invaluable price-index mentioned by Iris Green (p.84) and reproduced with the pullout map.

Some things have perhaps not changed as much as we think. Tony Noonan's exploration of Christianity in Penwith (chapter 12) paints a picture of thriving communities in numerous churches and chapels in the peninsula. He writes: 'The fact that there are nearly four thousand people attending a total of eighty-three places of Christian worship each Sunday hardly spells the end of Christianity,' and concludes: 'What divides Christians from each other seemed less important at the end of the century than at the beginning.' Emphasizing *what* people believe rather than *how* they express that belief, Tony tells a tale of continuity rather than change.

No one will argue about the changes in tin-mining, and Ron Hogg's short biography of Charles Harry (chapter 2) traces its boom and decline in the most vivid fashion: through its impact on people's lives. Harry was born and died in Carnyorth, near St Just, but in response to economic pressures he (with his brother) spent two substantial periods (1895-99 and 1910-17) working in South African mines, before ending his working life at Geevor in 1926. He died in 1939 aged 66, a good innings for a man in a very unhealthy trade. Even by then, two of the local mines he had worked in had shut (Botallack in 1914, Levant in 1930), and in 1990, Geevor closed, the last Penwith tin-mine. Mining is scat—but the St Just Mining District is now one of the ten locations which make up the Cornwall and West Devon World Heritage Site, conferring international recognition on its historical importance.[7]

Almost mirroring the collapse of mining was the rise of the West Cornwall artistic community. Pam Lomax' story of her house, Wheal Betsy (chapter 11), describes for us the networks of friends and relations which contributed to the decision of the Gotches (leading lights of the Newlyn artists' scene in the years before World War I) to build an Arts & Crafts house here. The overlapping circles of artists and architects was nationwide—although we learn for example that Tom Gotch's architect-brother knew Edward Prioleau Warren, the architect of the Fishermen's Mission in Newlyn, through the London-based Foreign Architectural Book Society—while the craftsmen who actually built the house were of course local: employed by Edward Pidwell of St James Street in Penzance. In the 1901 census, Mr Pidwell was a mason living with his family in Penare Terrace; but here he is in 1911, a builder and contractor, living at Green Bank and constructing important buildings.

Farming may be scat, but it is still central to the lives of many people in Penwith, especially those outside the towns of Penzance, Newlyn, St Just and St Ives. Jean Nankervis has farmed at Wicca in Zennor parish for nearly fifty years—but, as she would be the first to tell you, that must be set beside the amazing fact that there have been farmers at Wicca for *four thousand* years.[8] In chapter 5, Jean tells us the story of agriculture in West Cornwall through the reminiscences of a group of friends—'old codgers' who once ploughed with horses and lived in farmhouses with no running water, and who now drive combines and equip their houses with computers and freezers.

---

[6] See also John Loosemore's account of his school-days (below, p.36).

[7] See, for example, Cornish Mining World Heritage site.

[8] Nankervis.

In 1960 when I came to Zennor there were 28 dairy farms. ... Every farmer was a Zennor man or one of his relations, except at Trendrine. Now, in the year 2006, there is half that number of farmers because many have taken over neighbouring land. However, the same families run all but two of the farms.[9]

Continuity and change. John Loosemore quotes the adage: 'Live like you're going to die tomorrow, but farm like you're going to farm for ever.'[10]

At the start, I mentioned the great nineteenth-century innovations which affected the last century. That century's greatest impact on the world was arguably the idea and practice of total war. The Second World War affected Penwith at least as much as the First had, in good part because of the direct interest central government took in farming during those years, when feeding the British people was so difficult and so important. Jean's old codgers mention it, of course, but the main notice which this book takes of the war is in Susan Hoyle's record of a group of pacifists who farmed briefly around Nancledra. A sub-theme of this chapter (and also apparent in chapter 11 on Wheal Betsy) is the attraction which Penwith exerts on incomers, especially idealists and artists.

The pacifists had come together in an odd way, through the coincidence of several of them living in houses with blue doors, which the police feared were signals to the enemy. After Susan had finished writing her piece, another member of our history group mentioned the Nancledra pacifists to some friends, one of whom said: 'I remember them! They used to send messages to the Germans!' A little while later, Susan visited Higher Trenowin, a farm very close to several of the community's holdings, and the farmer there, Bridgette Clamp, showed her a barn-door painted blue—in the 1970s, sadly!—by her grandfather, who had however been there from long before the war, and painted many doors blue.

This is so often the way with historical research: you collect a document here, a book there, a treasure trove of an archive yonder—but it all falls into place only when you are able to plug into stray remarks which you almost ignored...

It is thanks to Iris Green that we chose the twentieth century. Iris pointed out that Penwith was in danger of losing an enormous amount of information about its relatively recent life and times if we, the local history group, neglected to do anything about it.

This was a big challenge, which we have done our best to meet. There are wonderful public archives (at the Morrab Library in Penzance, and for example at Truro's Courtney Library and County Record Office, as well as at the Cornwall Studies Centre in Redruth, and the National Archives at Kew). There are also private archives held by individuals—collections of letters, minutes, photographs, legal papers, books, ephemera—sometimes about their families, or their house, or parish; or about fishing, say, or Methodism, or artists. Then there are business papers, whose value to historians is often overlooked, or those of voluntary organizations. Most valuable perhaps, because most vulnerable, are people's memories—untrustworthy at times, goodness knows, but irreplaceably precious.

Our task has been to identify some of these rich sources, and to decide what we each would research and write about. Above all, we were satisfying our own curiosity as historians: what happened, and why? We have also been very aware that this is only a tiny fraction of what is there to be collected and understood. Almost any of the subjects treated in this book could have been expanded to fill the whole volume. And still so much has only been touched on if mentioned at all: tourism, for example, or local politics and government, or health....

We hope you enjoy this book, and find your own links to our recent past. Perhaps you will be inspired to make your own record of the twentieth century.

[9] Below, p.35.
[10] Below, p.37.

1. Penwith from the Sea: Reminiscences of a Fishery Officer

Glyn Richards

They that go down to the sea in ships that do business in great waters; these see the works of the Lord and his wonders in the deep. (Psalm 107: 23-24)

Before Cornwall's coastal patrol vessel service started in 1961, there was just one fishery officer who visited the many Cornish ports and coves by car. Often his job involved visiting just one or two small boats hauled up on a rocky slipway. His duties ranged from enforcing the fishery bye-laws, such as the minimum sizes of brown edible crabs allowed to be caught, to writing reports on planning applications where fishing interests were affected. The last of the early fishery officers was Cecil HB Richards. He had earlier been the skipper of the *Rosebud*, the famous little fishing boat that carried a petition from Newlyn to London in 1937 in an attempt to stop the demolition of cottages by Penzance Borough under their clearance scheme.

On 8 January 1965 I was appointed Fishery Officer and Engineer aboard the fisheries patrol vessel, *Cornubia*, based at Newlyn. The vessel patrolled the Cornwall Sea Fisheries District, which comprises 1350 nautical square miles of sea, originally three miles from the shore and now increased to six, stretching from Marsland Mouth near Bude on the north coast to Rame Head near Plymouth in the south. I was to spend the next thirty-six years responsible for the maintenance of the *Cornubia* and her three successors, while carrying out the duties of a fishery officer.

CORNUBIA: Service period, 1962-1973; length, 36 feet; construction, wood (mahogany on larch); crew, 2-3 fishery officers; cost, £10,000.

(Glyn Richards Collection)

PALORES: Service period, 1974-1991; length, 47 feet; construction, wood (iroko on American elm); crew, 3-4 fishery officers; cost, £50,000.

(Courtesy Eddie Downing)

VERIFIER: Service period, 1991-2000; length, 71 feet; construction, aluminium; crew, 4-5 fishery officers; cost, £300,000.

(Glyn Richards Collection)

SAINT PIRAN: Service period, 2000 to current; length, 88 feet; construction, aluminium; crew, 5-6 fishery officers; cost, £2.1 million.

(Glyn Richards Collection)

During that time, as a keen amateur photographer I recorded the changing scenes: the cliffs, wildlife, working fishermen and the many types of ships and unusual sights that passed by my unique platform on the patrol boat. In this brief chapter I describe some of the everyday scenes I encountered as we patrolled the coast of Penwith in the closing decades of the twentieth century. Our journey begins in Newlyn harbour aboard the *Saint Piran* at the start of a patrol while the engineers are going through their checklist in the engine room.

This is my view over the stern of the *Saint Piran* as we leave Newlyn Harbour and begin our trip around the coast of Penwith, February 2001. Generations of my family have lived and worked here and left me with a strong sense of belonging. (Glyn Richards Collection)

Early twentieth-century Mount's Bay luggers silently crossing Gwavas Lake on their way to the fishing grounds. As the men talk to each other across the decks, the only background noise is the creaking of the rigging and the lapping of the water against the hull. The age of plastics and man-made fibres is yet to come. The heavy brown sails are of treated cotton canvas and the natural fibre ropes of sisal and manilla. Fishing nets are of Egyptian cotton and the net floats are of cork imported from Spain. (Glyn Richards Collection; photographer unknown)

The first job is to start the diesel generator to provide power in the wheelhouse, the galley and just about everywhere else as these days most things are electrically operated and controlled. The main fuel tank levels are recorded, and the two main engines started and left to idle while we all help to bring in the fenders, let go and stow the mooring ropes as we slide away from the berth. Within a few minutes we round the lighthouse on the south pier, the same lighthouse that my great-grandfather, James Mann Hosking, would have known as he too left Newlyn in his Mount's Bay lugger *Our Jim* at the beginning of the twentieth century, quietly adjusting the sails to catch what wind there was in that tranquil world.

SG Harmer, in his recollections of the passing of the Cornish lugger, describes his feelings about the early twentieth-century change from sail to motor:

...it was my custom to stand at the end of Newlyn Pier and watch the unique and picturesque sight of the pilchard fleet slowly proceeding to sea for the night's fishing. The strength of the actual fleet varied from day to day but a rough estimate would perhaps place the number of vessels at over one hundred, including flotillas from the neighbouring

ports of St Ives, Porthleven and Mousehole. The excitement, bustle and agility with which the crews, arrayed in their snow white jumpers, hoisted the famous dark brown lug sails, mizzens and then manoeuvred for places as the little vessels rounded the lighthouse, attracted scores of visitors to the pier head and was the means of presenting many a brilliant picture to numerous artists... During the evenings of August 1921 it is again my custom to stand at the end of Newlyn

pier and watch the departure of the pilchard fleet. I see the same number of boats, the same sturdy crews in their snow white jumpers but the bustle, animation and excitement as the vessels round the lighthouse is absent. They now proceed to sea in single file like so many miniature destroyers the fascinating and bewitching dark brown lug sails have gone forever. The mainmasts are lowered as if in mourning and the constant throb, throb of the motor tells me that progress has once more robbed the world famous picture of its greatest charm.[11]

Pilchard Drivers *Peel Castle* and *Primrose* leaving Newlyn harbour, c1940s. (Morrab Library Collection)

As a boy, I remember the pilchard drivers *Peel Castle* and *Primrose* setting off on a summer's evening with their 'modern' petrol/paraffin engines, but these in turn have also been surpassed. Today's big beam trawlers can stay at sea for up to a week and, working further offshore, catch the prime bottom species such as monk, Dover sole, lemon sole, plaice, ray, megrim, brill and turbot.

Now back aboard *Saint Piran*, we pass the lighthouse into our offshore world and head across Gwavas Lake. We can immediately feel the heave of the deck beneath us, and the extremely noisy diesel engines are soon propelling us along at 18 knots. I remember my first trip, on 11 January 1965, when I was welcomed aboard the *Cornubia* by Clifton Pender, Chief Fishery Officer, and Reg Cooper, Assistant Fishery Officer. Mr Pender introduced me to *Cornubia*'s engines and equipment that I would come to know so well over the next nine years. 'Today', he suggested for my benefit, 'we should go for a short run to Porthcurno and back'. We left Newlyn that winter's day with a fresh south-west wind. Unlike most large fishing vessels, patrol boats with their shallow draught and high-speed diesel engines are uncomfortable and extremely noisy, especially when sea conditions worsen and there is a need to reduce speed. The *Cornubia* was only thirty-six feet in length with a wooden clinker-built hull, a canopy and open cockpit and, although perfectly seaworthy, was a rather lively lady travelling at about 12 knots with her twin 110 hp two-stroke diesel engines. I just managed to contain my breakfast on that first occasion.

As seafarers have known for centuries, Newlyn with its Gwavas Lake haven is strategically placed at the head of Mount's Bay. It is fifteen miles to the

PZ199 beam trawler the *Algrie* crossing Mount's Bay with her booms down for stability, September 2000. (Glyn Richards Collection)

The inshore trawler BM481 *Bethany James* towing along the western shore, 2001. The RIB from the *Saint Piran* keeps pace alongside and awaits the return of the boarding fishery officer. (Glyn Richards Collection)

---

[11] *Cornishman* and *Cornish Telegraph*, 17 August 1921.

Lizard Point and the south side of Cornwall and a similar distance to Land's End on the north coast, the direction in which we are heading on *Saint Piran* today. As the skipper settles the boat onto a steady course and the machinery warms up, I'm standing as I always do for those first few minutes, on the after-deck taking in the scenery. Two-and-a-half miles to the East is St Michael's Mount and as the bay sweeps around towards Penzance and Newlyn, Castle-an-Dinas hill is in the background and the coast of Penwith will unroll like a carpet before us. Close by we often see the Isles of Scilly ferry boat, *Scillonian III*. Her many passengers get a fine view of the coast here for a little while, until they head out towards the Wolf Rock lighthouse and St Mary's twenty-five miles south-west of Land's End and forty miles from Penzance.

Deep water along the western shore here allows *Saint Piran* close enough for us to see fine details of the coast. Penlee Quarry, a huge gash in the hillside, employed hundreds of men for over a century. Penlee Point was once the home of the local lifeboat until *Solomon Browne* was tragically lost with all hands in that terrible storm of 1981. Since then, our lifeboat has resided in Newlyn harbour. The lifeboat house at Penlee Point has been preserved and remains unchanged since that dreadful night.

Although *Saint Piran* is a large vessel, the tide is high so we can pass inside Mousehole Island (St Clement's Isle) and reduce speed to avoid our large bow wave wreaking havoc with the small punts or washing aggressively onto the beach. We have a fine view into the centre of the picturesque and historic Mousehole village. With a little imagination one can picture the scene on 23 July 1595 when four Spanish galleys suddenly arrived in Mount's Bay and 200 well-armed men came ashore. Having set alight the houses of Mousehole and Paul church, they moved on to Newlyn and Penzance, which met similar fates.

Tater Du Lighthouse

At times along our patrol, we stop and open the large hydraulic door in the stern to launch our RIB, the auxiliary boat. With two fishery officers aboard, it can intercept the various vessels, inspect their gear and catch. After centuries of freedom, fishermen have objected strongly to this relatively recent policing of their workplace, to being boarded, and to their catch and gear being inspected for any contravention. It is understandable that they sometimes feel this way, and I can relate especially to the older fishermen who have seen such large changes. To make matters worse, our jurisdiction in Cornish waters applied mainly to British Nationals operating vessels from Great Britain, Northern Ireland and the Channel Islands, and so at times anger, drawn from frustration, would be shown: 'Why don't you go and chase the Spanish or French and leave us alone?'

Having passed Mousehole, we are now approaching Lamorna Cove with its little stone jetty built to handle the granite from the long-disused and overgrown quarries. The same granite was used in the construction of the Thames Embankment in London long ago, some lighthouses, and the building of St Peter's Church at Newlyn in the early 1880s. Not far up the road from the cove, past the homes where once lived celebrated local artists, is the site of the famous Merry Maidens. This ancient circle of standing stones is said to be maidens turned to stone for dancing on the Sabbath. Two more standing stones nearby are the two fiddlers (other versions of the story relate them to be pipers), who took flight but still met the same fate.

The *Saint Piran* with its heavy wash trailing astern is now passing Tater Du Point and we keep off just far enough to avoid those isolated rocks called 'The Bucks'. Tater Du lighthouse, smaller than most, was built in 1965 (the year I joined the patrol service). According to Michael Tarrant,[12] the need for the lighthouse 'is clearly documented in any book about Cornish shipwrecks and the surprise is that the construction is not in 1865 instead'. Cornwall has a unique collection of lighthouses and when viewed from the sea they appear to me as works of art in their own right, a testimony to their builders.

The stretch of coast from Tater Du to Gwennap Head is less weather-beaten than other parts and therefore more accessible to the walker on the south-west coastal path. Once we pass Castle Treveen Point and the Logan Rock, we head in towards Porthcurno Head and along the shore.

I well remember one warm sunny afternoon in September 1999 aboard the *Verifier*, with a full

The Minack Theatre, Porthcurno, September 1999.
(Glyn Richards Collection)

Low tide at Porthgwarra Cove, August 2000.
(Glyn Richards Collection)

house at the Minack Theatre enjoying a matinee performance. The noise of *Verifier*'s 2000 hp diesel engines was reverberating off the cliff walls, and I hoped it did not distract the audience too much.

This world-famous open-air theatre was the inspiration of Rowena Cade in the early 1930s; the setting is spectacular and unique. Porthgwarra Cove is a little further on, tucked away between Porthcurno and Gwennap Head. In summertime when the tide is out holidaymakers enjoy themselves in the water, but the low tide leaves the fishing punts high and dry as they can only be launched and recovered when the tide is up on the slipway and with the aid of an electric winch.

The purse seiner PD90 *Accord* heading towards Land's End and probably bound for its home port Peterhead, Scotland, after the Cornish mackerel season, December 1997. (Glyn Richards Collection).

---

[12] Tarrant. For full bibliographical details, see the Bibliography on pp. 113-116.

Small 'covers' can often be seen along the shore near the Runnelstone buoy, fishing for mackerel and bass. As a twelve-year-old boy with my grandfather we caught mackerel one at a time from our small punt, but since then I have seen catching methods increase with technology until the arrival of the purse seiner, the ultimate in catching power. Weighing about 205 tons and around 47 metres long, the purse seiner is capable of taking catches of around 360 tons of the pelagic species that shoal and swim in the mid-water depths, for example mackerel, pilchard and herring. The shoals are located by sonar and the huge net, capable of encompassing St Paul's Cathedral, is shot in a large circle and the bottom drawn in like a purse. The fish are then pumped aboard into large, chilled seawater tanks.

There is not too much tide on our journey today, so with local knowledge and the advice handed down to us from fishermen of the past, *Saint Piran* is able to pass inside the Runnelstone Rocks and under Gwennap Head and then open up our next course to Land's End. The coastline here is made up of austere, craggy and menacing cliffs, topped with grand, windswept open moorland.

The St Ives reserve lifeboat, Royal Shipwright, pictured between Gwennap Head and Land's End, February 1998. Coxswain Tommy Cocking is believed to be at the helm. There have been thousands of shipwrecks on this peninsula with countless lives lost over centuries, with no particular safe harbour refuge on the north coast. There are three all-weather lifeboats around Penwith, with their dedicated crews supported by rescue helicopters during emergencies. (Glyn Richards Collection).

A common dolphin keeping pace with his friends, just under the bow of the *Palores* travelling at twelve knots, off the Longships, Land's End, December 1987. You can see the side fender and bow wash of *Palores* and the clouds reflected in the water. (Glyn Richards Collection).

Now is as good a time as any along our journey to mention the marine wildlife common to Penwith's coastline. Dolphins, porpoises, basking sharks, pilot whales and Atlantic seals are some of the many creatures I have seen over the years.

The birdlife is also rich: cormorants standing on the rocks with wings outstretched drying in the sun; diving, darting guillemots, razorbills and streamlined gannets with their cream heads and black wing-tips; the occasional storm petrel (sometimes referred to as 'Mother Carey's chicken') fluttering above us in the darkness; and of course the noisy and ever-present seagull.

Some species, for example the dolphins and basking sharks, can suddenly appear in great numbers after somewhat lean years. These days some might say that global warming is the cause of such happenings, although after fifty years observing the scene I tend to think that this is the natural order of things.

The cliffs at Land's End are the face that Penwith presents to the Atlantic Ocean and the prevailing south-west winds. From here we head due north, passing Sennen Cove and the beautiful stretch of sandy shore known as Whitesand Bay. It was at Sennen on 7 September 1497 that pretender Perkin Warbeck landed from Cork, Ireland, with a force of men, proclaiming himself to be Richard IV. There was little support for his cause from the local people, who had experienced the disastrous outcome of their own Cornish Rebellion earlier the same year. The little church at Sennen, one mile from Land's End, dates from the thirteenth century with possible origins back to 520 AD. It reminds me of other ancient church towers across Penwith visible from the sea that ships' pilots have used as landmarks over the centuries. Soon we are abeam of 'The Brisons', that rocky islet one mile off Cape Cornwall, the only 'cape' in England. This is real mining country, with the old workings along the coast towards St Ives bearing famous names such as Levant, Geevor and Botallack. Botallack mine near St Just had workings that extended outwards 2,500 feet under the sea.

Land's End Hotel, the 'last hotel in England', perched atop this most westerly tip of England appears to mariners down below like a doll's house, February 2000.
(Glyn Richards Collection)

Past Pendeen and approaching Gurnard's Head you will see Bosigran and Porthmeor cove. Rising above them across the road are the slopes leading up to the rocky Carn Galver at the top, well worth the climb for the fabulous view. On a fine day, perhaps continue on from here across the moors to Ding Dong and the hamlet of Newmill. Watch out for the occasional adder sunning itself on the rocky path, though it should slither away at the sound of your approach.

The famous Crowns Mine of Botallack, February 2000. Early photographs show the complex timber support structures, now long gone, perched precariously on the cliff's edge. (Glyn Richards Collection)

There is more spectacular scenery along this next stretch of shoreline and fishermen set their crab pots right up close to the base of the cliffs. The much sought-after bass is often caught here by local boats, and from ashore by anglers off the rocks. The boarding officers witness this first hand from their smaller craft while the *Saint Piran* stands off at a safe distance and awaits their return. Our view from seaward sweeps up the valley to Zennor moors and isolated farms until the road disappears behind Eagle's Nest, an isolated house perched on the hillside. I have memories of summer holidays there as a child in the 1940s when my aunt and uncle were employed there as housekeeper and gardener. The area has a certain feeling of mysticism and timelessness and draws artists and authors.

Will Arnold-Forster once lived there, his visitors including Ethiopia's last emperor, Haile Selassie, and Ivor Novello. Author DH Lawrence and his wife lived in a cottage below the hill. Then, with Zennor Head disappearing astern, we come up to the rocks called 'The Carracks', referred to locally as Seal Island and home to Atlantic grey seals.

Small inshore fishing boat SS170 *Jen* in St Ives Bay, March 2000. Local fisherman Simon Rouncefield in the stern and the young crewman in the bow are cleaning gill nets. Fishery officer Simon Cadman (centre) has been put aboard from the Saint Piran to hear 'the news'. (Glyn Richards Collection)

Moving on we have sightings of fishing vessels of various shapes and sizes. We see 'toshers' along the shore, hand-lining for mackerel and bass; other small boats working pots for brown crab, lobsters and spider crabs; small inshore trawlers fishing for the demersal species, those fish that live and feed on or near the bottom, such as cod, haddock, whiting, pollock, gurnard and plaice; further off there are larger trawlers and other vessels that may not fish in our district because of restrictions.

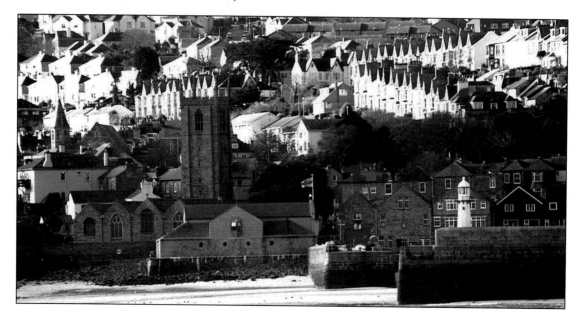

St Ives from the sea at low tide, showing St Eia Church, the lighthouse and the harbour entrance, January 1999. (Glyn Richards Collection)

We are approaching St Ives, its artists' colony and fine sandy beaches and branch line link to St Erth. It includes Porthmeor, facing north for the surfers with the Tate Gallery above the beach. Around St Ives Head, or The Island, is the more sheltered Porthminster Beach. We have reached the end of our journey around Penwith. With the tide out this is as close as we can get with *Saint Piran* without running aground. We are continuing farther up the north coast, so we must put our passengers ashore in the RIB. I suggest you ride back to Penzance using the coast road and complete your picture of coastal Penwith—but do remember that we have seen Penwith from the sea on a fine day. Be mindful of the many periods of bad weather, the storms and the awesome sea conditions that so often assail our Peninsula, the tragedies and the loss of life there have been, even today in spite of technology and all the modern aids to navigation.

We hope you have enjoyed the trip; it has been a pleasure having you aboard.

2. A Migrant Miner from St Just at the Turn of the Twentieth Century
Ron Hogg

In 1856, when Cornwall's copper-ore production peaked at 164,000 tons, it was the most important metal mining region in Britain, accounting for over half of UK output, and a world force in steam power and deep lode, hard rock technology. By 1913, copper production had dwindled to an insignificant 420 tons... In the 1850s, some 36,500 men, women and children, over a quarter of the entire local labour force, worked at the mines. By 1911, employment, now almost entirely male, had gone down to 7,600, or six per cent of total Cornish employment. Mining failure was associated with increased out-migration: in every decade from the 1860s to the early 1900s, some twenty per cent of the male working population departed for overseas, three times the average for England and Wales.[13]

This paper is constructed around the life of Charles Harry, a miner from Carnyorth near St Just who lived from 1872 until 1939. His story is used as a device for selecting and exploring aspects of mining in Cornwall between the end of the nineteenth century and the early years of the twentieth century. In this way the paper links a local history perspective with the theoretical perspectives of mining history.

Charles Harry worked down the mines of Levant, Botallack and Geevor (see map, *right*), which were all part of the St Just mining area and less than three quarters of a mile from Carnyorth where he was born on 11 October 1872 and where he eventually died in 1939. Like many miners from the St Just area at this time in history, Charles Harry was a migrant worker who was forced to travel far from home in order to earn his living.

Map of St Just Mines (P.L.)

The migrant worker was a by-product of mining in Cornwall; the history of St Just explains the phenomenon well. From a small settlement of farms and cottages surrounding a parish church, St Just was transformed into a small industrial town by a massive mining boom in the 1820s. The population increased from 2,779 in 1800 to 7,048 in 1841, and the number of inhabited houses from 536 to 1,282.[14] Within the district, hamlets like Carnyorth grew into substantial settlements whose occupants worked almost exclusively in the mines. The boom continued until the 1860s, when mining went into decline in Cornwall, and by the close of the century, nearly all mining had moved away from the immediate environs of St Just. Fortunately, the St Just mines had achieved world renown as pioneer submarine mines, and the miners, expert in deep hard-rock technologies, had developed important skills. This led to a strong demand for their services from overseas, and encouraged them to become migrant workers. The fall in the population of St Just parish from more than 9,000 in 1861 to just over 5,500 in 1901 was almost definitely the result of emigration.[15]

Charles Harry was listed as a scholar in the 1881 census, and while this might have meant that he attended Sunday school, it is more likely that he attended the Board School in Pendeen. If so, Charles was lucky because there were more children than school places in the parish and some could not go to school. Perhaps it helped that the family lived at 'Carnyorth Moor, down the side of the school' (1881 census). The Education Act of 1870 did not make school compulsory for boys under twelve but it did exclude them from working underground, so in 1884, when he started work at the age of eleven, he

---

[13] Perry: 3. For full bibliographical details, see the Bibliography on pp. 113-116.
[14] Courtney: 92.
[15] Cahill: 8-9.

became a surface worker at the local Levant mine. He followed in the footsteps of his parents, as his father was a tin dresser (1891 census) and his mother a balmaiden.

Charles Harry (Courtesy Carlene Harry)

On his first day, Charles Harry joined the exodus of miners from Carnyorth to start the early shift. Miners from the surrounding area congregated on the crossroads at the bottom of Nancherrow Hill on their long walk to the mines. Carnyorth was closer to Levant, and Charles followed the 'well trodden paths leading between gorse bushes and bracken, eventually hearing the familiar sounds of creaking flat rods and the rattle of geared wheels of the man engine, bringing up the night shift.'[16] Levant was an amalgamation of several much more ancient mines, notably, Wheal Shap, Wheal Unity, Zawnbrinny and Boscregan. When Charles started work it was under new management, having been taken over the previous year when 2,500 new shares were issued. It was reported that '£11 per share was immediately disbursed in resuscitating the mine, and while this was in progress, the lords magnanimously gave up the usual dues—a piece of consideration gratefully acknowledged by the adventurers.'[17]

At this time most mines were run as cost-book companies which were financed by 'adventurers'. The adventurers were the shareholders with unlimited liability who were paid dividends in proportion to the number of shares they held. When more money was required a 'call' could be made on the adventurers.[18] It was well known that the adventurer sometimes reaped immense profits for a small outlay, 'and this being bruited abroad encouraged others to speculate; while like most gamblers' they were 'generally silent about their losses'. It was also said that the working miner liked a little speculation, and though he always worked hard for little gain, he always lived in hope.[19]

The cost-book system was almost universal at this time (it was to last at Levant until 1920) but its disadvantage was that the mine never built up capital and had no reserves in time of need, one of the reasons for the volatility in the industry where mines opened and closed frequently.[20] The old Levant Company had employed about 600 persons, but this was much reduced in 1883, the new company employing 82 men and 48 girls and boys as surface workers, and 216 men and 20 boys underground. The average wage of underground workers was £3/15/0d a month for men and £1-£2 a month for boys, and for surface workers £3 a month for men and 10/- a month for boys and girls.[21] So this is what Charles Harry would have earned.

Corin[22] describes the way the mine was managed at this time. A committee of management was appointed from the adventurers; there was an office headed by the purser, the managing agents or mine-captains; and there were the miners. The new management of 1882 had been the result of a disagreement between the management committee and the mine-captains. The mine-captains were the practical men who had hands-on experience. In 1882 the two most senior mine-captains had resigned and three new mine-agents, Captains Newton, Nankervis and Trembath, had been appointed. The 'office' remained intact with Major Dick White, who was said to have never been below ground, as purser.

---

[16] Langworthy: 2.
[17] EW Crofts (under the pen name, Ouit), *Cornishman*, 13 December 1883.
[18] Noall 1970: 45.
[19] Buller: 9.
[20] Guthrie: 68.
[21] Crofts (Ouit), *Cornishman*, 13 December 1883.
[22] Corin: 4, 18-19.

It was fortunate for Charles Harry that he started work at a time when old machinery was being replaced and the surface works were being improved. In charge was the 'Grass Captain', who oversaw all the surface work. Levant was a large mine and the most prominent building was the engine house, containing the pumping engine which was driven by steam and was remarkably silent. Croft described 'the almost noiseless rise and fall of the engine bob', 'the gurgle and hiss of the water in the pumps', and 'the splash of the little rivulet, red and warm, which was forced up to the surface'.[23] Nearby, a little engine house perched on the edge of the cliff, housed a 27' cylinder winding engine or whim which was employed to raise the ore to the surface and took the place of swinging buckets worked by horses, which had been used at one time at Levant. As well as the pumping engine and the beam engine, there were engines to drive the stamps, and a mill area with rag frames and buddles. Charles Harry probably took a turn on the dressing floor where his task would have been to wash the mud from the stamps in order to separate out the metallic particles, a process known as 'buddling'. Once separated, the metallic particles, containing tin, copper and arsenic, were returned to a calciner or furnace to roast the ore, where the arsenic was driven off in white poisonous fumes and the tin and copper when cooled could be sorted by the 'dresser'. A new calciner had been part of the recent 'resuscitation'.[24]

The treatment of the copper was a job that was given to women and boys. The copper ore was first broken up by women known as balmaidens, then it was re-sorted and made into fine gravel, after which it was 'jigged' or cleaned by shaking in a sieve under water, a job given to boys. The balmaidens' job was little different from forty years earlier, when the Rev[d] Buller described them as 'females toiling, like slaves, from morn to night, to gain a hard earned pittance', and explained that while some were forced to work because of poverty at home, others did so 'to gratify their vanity, and display their goodly figure in a costly dress on the approaching holiday'.[25]

Underground at Levant Mine, 1890s (Courtesy LJ Bullen)

Non-mining people considered these women to be disreputable and there was a saying that the language the balmaidens used was as black as their aprons were white. In fact the balmaidens only wore their clean, starched white aprons for walking out or photographs. Working with tin and copper ore was a messy business and their working costume consisted of protective leg, arm and hand covering and a hessian 'towser' or apron. Charles' mother was a balmaiden and she could have worked at Levant when he started there in 1884. Certainly his future sister-in-law (Mary Bennetts Rowe) was a balmaiden working at nearby Carnyorth mine.[26]

In 1887, Charles (aged 15) graduated to underground work. By then some of the shafts in the mine had reached a depth of 278 fathoms below adit and were to continue to go deeper during his time there, reaching 326 fathoms by 1900.[27] The old system had been to descend the mines using ladders when miners might climb 1,200 feet a day, which equalled the maximum permitted on a prison treadmill! Charles was fortunate in that a 'man engine' had been installed in one of the shafts in 1856,

[23] Crofts (Ouit), *Cornishman,* 29 December 1883.
[24] Noall 1970: 53
[25] Buller: 55
[26] Mayers: 165-167.
[27] Noall 1970: 14

reached by a tunnel from the miner's dry (the miners' changing room). This reduced the journey time from surface to the workings below, which was less tiring for the men and more profitable for the shareholders. The man engine consisted of a huge wooden rod that at Levant descended into the shaft for 1,600 feet. Platforms (or steps) for men to stand on were fixed at twelve-foot intervals along the length of the rod with corresponding platforms (or sollars) built into the sides of the shaft. An engine at the top of the shaft drove the wooden rod up and down with a stroke of twelve feet so that a man could stand on the step at a higher level and get off onto the sollar twelve feet below, and so on until he reached the end of the rod at the bottom of the shaft.

On his first day underground Charles would have had to go to the miner's dry to change into the clothes that miners wore underground. These included a bowler hat stiffened with resin, and Charles would have fixed a handful of wet clay on the front of his hat to make a holder for his candle. Charles Harry's nephew Raymond Harry worked at Levant from 1916, and under the pen name Jack Penhale,

Man Engine, 1900 (Courtesy LJ Bullen)

he wrote a description of his first descent on the man engine under the wing of the more experienced Will, which must have been very similar to that experienced by the young Charles Harry.

'The step is here ...right, step on.' Jack grasps the iron handle which is attached to the rod about four feet above every step, and his feet find the step, rather clumsily. Will glides in behind him on the same step. 'Don't grip the handle too tightly,' he warns, as they begin to go down. 'Right, step off,' he says, as, the rod reaches the bottom of its 12-foot stroke, and Jack is guided on to the sollar by Will. Another step comes up. 'Step on,' and again Jack grasps the handle, steps on, and is plunged down another 12 feet. 'Step off.' Up goes the step they have just left, and up comes another from below. 'Step on.' They drop down another 12 feet. 'Step off, step on, step off.' Their only illumination now is that supplied by their candles, and Will tells Jack to watch for the handle instead of looking for the step. It is by the feel of the handle that the miner can tell when the engine has reached the top of its stroke and Jack, grasping the handle, begins to feel, too, that momentary hesitancy before the rod begins to descend again.[28]

The descent continued until the 266-fathom level. The photograph on the left is an underground-view of the man engine shaft with the rod of the engine on the right with the hand grip. The step on which the miner stood is just below the feet of the central figure. The 'knocker line' handle is in the centre of the photograph. This wire line ran through the depth of the shaft and was used to signal the driver of the engine at surface.[29]

Levant yielded copper and tin, and its workings extended 2,000 feet out below the sea. When Charles worked at the higher levels, he could hear 'the awful grandeur of the rounded boulders rolling over his head as they are driven forwards and backwards by the force of the coming and receding waves.'[30] He would have learned caution when stoping above the 40 fathom level, which was as close to the sea bed as was safe to go, particularly if he was near the notorious spot known as the '40 backs'. He would have become familiar with the many strange noises, which miners identified as Knockers,

---

[28] Penhale: 15-16.
[29] Bullen: 51.
[30] Buller: 53

unpredictable pixies who might lead miners to rich lodes or to sudden death. Visitors to the mine often fled in panic when they first heard the sound of the sea, much to the miners' merriment.

Charles also worked underground at nearby Botallack. This was an even older mine than Levant and included, besides the old Botallack mine, the Crowns section and Wheal Cock (which were worked below the sea), and the Carnyorth mine. The celebrated Diagonal Shaft in the Crowns section was sunk for 2,616 feet at an angle of 32.5 degrees from the horizontal and the workings extending 1,360 feet beneath the sea. Botallack mine had been the richest tin-mine in Cornwall but in March 1895, the price of tin fell and the mine closed down.[31] Many families from St Just were threatened with destitution and so the men sought work abroad.

During the 1890s Cornish miners flocked to the Witwatersrand in the South African Transvaal because of high wages. 'News from Foreign Mining' regularly appeared in the *Cornishman* reporting on conditions in South African mines, where certain jobs were reserved for whites and the small group of skilled white miners was paid high wages: £18 to £22 a month.[32] As times worsened at home, money from abroad kept many families from penury. As one contemporary wrote:

> *The mine was the soul of the moor, and the pumps and stamps its music. The young men now are spread over South Africa and Australia, South America and the regions of Klondike; and the old people and young wives and children are left at home, dependent for daily bread upon the love of kindred whom they might never see again.[33]*

In 1895 Charles Harry was supporting his parents and younger sister, while his brother William (Willie) had a pregnant wife. That year, Willie left for South Africa and Charles followed one year later. The journey to South Africa from St Just followed a well traversed route. Every Friday morning the 'up-train' included special cars labelled 'Southampton', the embarkation port for South Africa. The migrants travelled via Plymouth, and if they were sailing on the Union Line Mail Steamers, their train ticket from Plymouth to Southampton was paid by the shipping line.

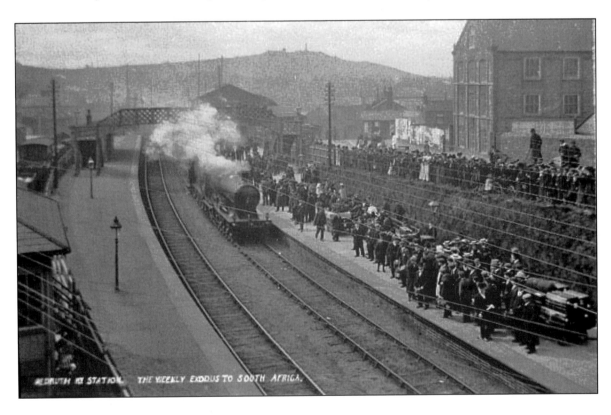

Redruth Station - the weekly exodus to South Africa (Courtesy Cornish Studies Library)

---

[31] Trounson: 57-59.
[32] Nauright: 14.
[33] Payton: 350.

The picture on the previous page shows men awaiting the train for the boat to South Africa at Redruth station. A similar crowd would be at the station at Camborne. It was a rare sight, we are told:

At Camborne station of a Friday the platforms'd be packed with a great crowd of people, laughin', cryin', shoutin' ... Then the train would steam in slowly and there'd be a great rush for the special carriages labelled 'Southampton'. Then there'd be kissin' and shakin' and she'd move out, leaving the womenfolk and the children wavin' and sobbin'.[34]

One cannot doubt the importance of the South African mining industry to Cornwall at this time. The two-way traffic of Cornish skilled labour to South Africa, and 'the eagerly awaited funds flowing in the opposite direction' meant that Cornwall 'was spared the worst ravages of mass unemployment' and 'developed an informal welfare system or dependency culture of hitherto unparalleled proportions, in which the well-being of large sections of the community in places such as Redruth or St Just-in-Penwith was reliant upon the efforts of Cornish miners in South Africa'.[35]

It seems likely that Charles Harry was quickly welcomed into one of the many Cornish networks that existed in the Rand and he was soon at work. Between July 1896 and September 1899 he worked in the Transvaal at New Blue Sky & Cinderella mines, Borksburg and Geldenhuis [Glenhuis] Main Reef & New Herriot mines, GM Co. During this time he acquired new skills, such as those associated with a blasting certificate, dated 15 December 1896 (Harry Family Archive). He would also have had time for enjoyment and must have visited Johannesburg which was the centre of the Rand and according to C. Lewis Hind, 'but a suburb of Cornwall'. Here he would have found many cousin Jacks, some of whom he would have known in Cornwall. He might have had the traditional Cornish pasty at Mrs Dooney's boarding house where 200 Cornish miners might sit down to a Sunday meal. Both Harry brothers were typical of the migrants identified as 'single roving miners', who, if married, left their wife and family in Cornwall, and who (married or single) returned to Cornwall as often as possible either to work or while 'en route' to another part of the world.

The Cornish were particularly important on the Rand at this time.

By 1899 there were nine major companies managing more than 100 mines. (...) In perhaps as many as a third of the principal gold-mines almost all of the white employees were Cornish, with experienced Cousin Jack miners earning between £6 and £9 per week, a far cry from the £3 per month that was then the going rate in Cornwall (...) St Just men continued to be prominent. John Rowe was manager of the Central Langlaagte mine and Solomon James was captain of the George Goch. James Matthews, also from St Just, was at the Worcester, and Nicholas Williams ran the Knights Deep. Other Cornish captains included John Pope, from Breage, who was at the Glenhuis mine until 1895.[36]

Unfortunately this situation was soon to end. The outbreak of the Boer War forced Charles and Willie Harry to return to Carnyorth at the end of 1899. In that year, there were 10,266 white miners employed in South Africa along with 96,709 Africans.[37] Many miners returned to Cornwall because of the war, for example fifty of the repatriates were taken on at Levant in February 1900. It was not an auspicious time to return home as tin-prices were at an all-time low and many of St Just mines had closed. People had come to rely on South Africa as 'a sort of outlying farm for the mining division'.[38] When things were brisk there, every mail brought twenty or thirty thousand pounds sterling for folk at home, but during the Boer War most of the shops were in mourning, and people went about with hunger in their eyes. Charles Harry was still a bachelor and his remittance home would have gone to his parents. The 1901 census shows Charles living at Carnyorth with his father Charles (aged 60), his mother Elizabeth (aged 55) and his sister Maggie (aged 17). Willie, on the other hand, was married, and his son William had been born in 1896, while he was still in South Africa working at the New Primrose Gold Mine in the Transvaal (Harry Family Archive). His second child Mary was born in 1900, after Willie had returned to Cornwall, and the 1901 census shows the four of them as a single household. This clearly demonstrates the new pattern of family life that was emerging as a result of migration. There was a decreased birth-rate leading to smaller nuclear households. Some women moved in with family while

---

[34] Nauright: 13-14.
[35] Payton: 350
[36] Payton: 359
[37] Levy: 82; quoting the Chamber of Mines Annual Report.
[38] Noall 1970: 91.

their husbands were abroad, and sometimes two or more female-headed households merged together. In the worst-case scenario an unfortunate woman and her children would become destitute and be forced to approach the Board of Guardians for relief.[39]

Charles and Willie Harry must have done reasonably well in South Africa because in 1900 they became partners in a new venture, Chellew, Troon & Co. There were twelve partners: Stephen Troon, Joseph Chellew, Henry Troon, William Casley, Charles Troon, James Troon, Andrew Angwin, Thomas Grose, Thomas R Wall, Henry Semmens, William T. Harry and Charles Harry. The company crushed the waste from abandoned mines, working at Botallack Moor, Wheal Owles, Wheal Cock and Carnyorth Moor. It was hands-on work for the partners. The waste was sampled by vanning shovel and transported by horse and cart (this cost 6s per day for six loads) to Nancherrow or the Kenidjack Valley where it was crushed and dressed. The photograph on the right shows Charles and Willie Harry when they were working the waste dumps.

Charles Harry, Willie Harry, Ned Wall & Tom Wall c. 1902
Courtesy Carlene Harry

As well as this work, the partners (all miners) also worked several of the old shaft pillars above adit, which was dangerous work but financially rewarding (Harry Family Archive).

Like many single men returning from a spell in South Africa, Charles found a bride, Lillie Evelyn Stevens, and they were married at Trewellard Methodist Chapel on 23 April 1902. Lillie had been born in Colorado and was ten years younger than her husband. She was the daughter of migrant Cornish parents from Carnyorth and Sancreed, who had eventually returned to their roots. After their marriage Charles and Lillie lived with Lillie's mother at Wesley House, where she did the housekeeping for them. Maybe his new marital status was inspiration for Charles to better himself, and in1902-1903, he attended Pendeen Evening Classes. His exercise book (still in the family archive) suggests he was an able student. His first child Lilian was born in 1903, followed by Charles Clifford in 1904 and Winston Stevens in 1909. It is interesting that Charles and Lillie did not want their children to go down the mines, and their eldest son, Charles Clifford, became a schoolteacher.[40]

In 1909 the partnership ended and Charles Harry and his brother became migrant workers again. They left for South Africa in 1910. During this time the brothers returned home from time to time, but never together, either because they looked after each others' interests in South Africa or so that their families had the support of one or other of them more often than if they had returned together. However Cornish women had always had a major role in the division of labour working as balmaidens in the mines, so they adapted easily to their new responsibilities of domestic control at home while their men worked overseas.

Charles & Lillie with daughter, c1903
(Courtesy Carlene Harry)

The caring miners looked after not only their wives and children but often their elderly parents as well. Charles Harry sent money to his parents each month and when the grandchildren went to visit,

---

[39] Payton: 351
[40] Interview with Carlene Harry, August 2006

they never went empty-handed, taking 'a large jug of broth with ample beef, leeks, onions and other vegetables that were in season' or 'a heavy, saffron or seed cake' or 'an apple or blackberry tart'. In 1910 there was correspondence about the brothers buying their father a new suit.[41] Meanwhile the miners abroad had to entertain themselves. A glimpse of Charles' life in South Africa is given in the extract of a letter he wrote in 1911.

> *Coronation day will be over before you get this letter but I hope that everybody at home will have a very enjoyable day. How we shall celebrate it out here I don't know. I don't hear much about it on the mine. I expect we shall have to work as usual. Most mines on the Rand have Reading Rooms in connection with them but we haven't one here and because of that hardly know what is taking place out here or at home and after being used to seeing the paper every day one feels at a loss to be without it.*[42]

Reproduced above is Charles Harry's employment record 1910-1917. Charles worked as a hand stoper at Langlaagte until the end of June1911. Coincidentely, Phyllis Gotch visited this mine six weeks later. According to Phyllis, the mine-captain was a big handsome Cornishman and the manager was Hebbard, the Cornishman who signed Charles Harry's employment record. Phyllis was very like the independent Cornish women with whom she had grown up and insisted on going underground. She described her experience in a letter to her parents.

> *'We motored off to a mine called Longlottie (sic)... The manager there is called Hebbard and comes from Cornwall and most of the men are Cornish...I asked to see the working part of the mine not the show part...I am the first woman who ever went down below the levels the skip goes down to—the first woman to go right down to the bottom—the 17th level and all through it: the climb is very difficult, wet and murky and the mine-captain said I fair astonished him...But my word it was hard work—and climbing up, the stones give way beneath us and slide with you—no white men do actual work there it is too hot—but black boys almost stark nude work and it is lighted by electric light—great Scott I was astonished—it is all a wonderful series of pictures—but the sound of the air pumps going and the drills give you the queerest feeling. The white men look all deadbeat and half of them get their lungs bad...the flying dust and sudden change from heat to bitter cold...It is one of the hardest lives that men can live'*[43]

Ernest Patrick Doherty (later to marry Phyllis Gotch) was also in Johannesburg in 1911. Before going to South Africa Doherty was trained at Camborne School of Mines, which according to Phyllis was 'child's play' compared to the real thing. Doherty had to begin at the bottom and really rough it— up at six, clean out his own room, underground in heat, cold and dust, and standing up to his knees in water for hours at a time. 'No excuses were taken and no difference was made between a Cambridge

---

[41] Interview with Carlene Harry
[42] Letter from Charles Harry to TS Newall, 9 June 1911. Harry Family Archive
[43] Letter from Phyllis Gotch to her parents, August 1911. Wheal Betsy Archive

man (like Doherty) and a cockney from the East End', wrote Phyllis.[44] Phyllis and Doherty married in South Africa and although she returned just before the outbreak of war, he was left in South Africa where he died of phthisis, a disease particularly prevalent in the dust-filled stopes of the South African mines.[45]

When war was declared on 5 August 1914, Charles was working at Nigel GM Co. Despite the great difficulty returning home at this time, both brothers got away from Transvaal before the end of the war, Willie leaving in 1915 and Charles on 24 December 1917. Willie left because he was seriously ill, the years underground having taken their toll on his health. 'Yes, it's dust on the lungs', Raymond Harry wrote later, 'not just ordinary dust, but fine sharp dust of quartz, which floats in the air in the African mines.'[46] Raymond, who was Willie's son, would have known, because Willie was to die at the age of 45 in 1917 before Charles Harry got home. Although Charles was no longer a young man, and also suffered from 'dust on the lungs', his return to Carnyorth was probably determined by the state of the South African mining industry. Even before the war, cheap Chinese labour was imported in preference to the more expensive skilled white workforce. After the war this deskilling continued with mine-owners preferring to employ the abundant cheap African labour available.

Langlaagte Deep Gold Mine - Machine Driving or Cutting Tunnel about 1,100 feet (Gotch Family Archive)

When Charles Harry started work at Geevor in March 1918, it looked like the photograph below, which was taken just after the end of the First World War and shows the terminal station of the aerial ropeway from Wethered Shaft, and some of the mill buildings. In the foreground is a pair of winding drums that were part of the steam-winding engine erected on the Victory Shaft sunk to commemorate the Allies' victory in 1918.[47] Geevor Tin mine was one of the last mines to open in the St Just district.

Geevor Mine, 1918 (Courtesy LJ Bullen)

---

[44] Letter from Phyllis Gotch, Victoria Hotel, Jo'burg to her parents, 7 August 1911. Wheal Betsy Archive
[45] Jenkin: 330.
[46] Penhale: 7
[47] Bullen: 55

There had been mining at Geevor before but in 1905 the West Australian Gold Fields Company acquired the mining rights, opening the mine under the name North Levant and Geevor Ltd. In 1911 the mine was renamed Geevor Tin Mines Ltd, and included North Levant, Geevor, Wheal Carne and Wheal Bal.

Charles Harry must have blessed his luck that he was working at Geevor and not Levant when eighteen months after his return from South Africa, the last remaining man engine in Cornwall broke just as the shift change was taking place on Monday, 20 October 1919. Thirty-one men died and many were injured. Charles Harry's nephew was working underground at Levant and was one of the few to escape. Later, he recorded his lucky escape:

Jack joins the other young men...These young men from these upper levels are in a hurry to get up, and they climb the ladders in the pumping shaft as far as possible before catching the engine... About twenty of these youngsters make their way upwards. Bound for the 130, 120 or even 100 fathom level. This has become a daily habit, and this habit today is to be the means of saving their lives ... but they do not know this as yet. Jack decides to make for the 120, as he decides that this level offers as good a chance as any to catch the engine...Almost imperceptibly the engine starts to move, slowly, very slowly, as the driver gives her steam in her cylinder...She picks up speed, the step is down; Jack is on, and upward bound...Silently the engine lifts the men, for there is no fuss with her as she glides smoothly up and down. Up, keep on, upwards, step after step. ...what is that quiver that seems to be travelling through the rod? Is she getting tired of this everlasting bobbing up and down; or is it just imagination? Yet as we go higher, the quiver, the tremble, the vibration, seem to be plainer. But the first riders are young, and cannot be bothered about this. They are too inexperienced to know that this vibration should not be here. Chatting and laughing, they rise higher and higher, until, at last, they reach the tunnel here they leave the engine and go upwards towards the day. They have escaped the holocaust by about one minute.[48]

Another account reads:

Just prior to the accident the engine was working normally, going 4¼ strokes per minute. At ten minutes to three in the afternoon it suddenly jumped to a faster speed, continued at that rate for three quarters of a revolution, and then stopped altogether. Trembath immediately reversed the engine and shut off the steam; he acted promptly and correctly under the circumstances, but the damage had already been done, and could not have been averted by any action on his part. The rod at that moment was fully loaded with men, and thus formed a 'human pillar' extending from the top to bottom of the shaft. An instant more, and all these miners would have stepped off and paused on the sollars to await the next up-stroke of the engine, in which case few or no lives would have been lost. But this was not to be. The flawed iron snapped, releasing its tremendous burden, and down crashed the structure in a mass of debris and wreckage.[49]

Charles Harry probably rushed to Levant from Geevor to help the rescue operation. Few families in St Just escaped the consequences of this disaster, although from Carnyorth only Thomas Branwell died. The Branwells lived next door to Charles and Lillie, and Lillie broke the news to Mrs Branwell. Charles Harry's lasting memory of that awful day was of the utter silence; it was the first time in his life that no mine was working and the stamps were quiet.[50] Charles continued to work at Geevor until May 1926, mainly working underground as a stoper, with occasional breaks for illness and one longer break when Geevor mine closed down due to the post-war slump between February 1921 and January 1922. When he finally retired in 1926, Charles was 53, and was to live another 13 years until he was 66. Not a bad age for a man whose life had spanned the turn of the twentieth century and who had spent much of that life underground. In fact the mines in which he spent his working life were not to last much longer, Botallack closing in 1914, Levant in 1930 and Geevor in 1990.

---

[48] J Penhale, p7

[49] HA Abbott, HM Inspector of Mines, *Mining Magazine*, Vol 22, 1920, reproduced in Noall 1970:113-114.

[50] Interview with Carlene Harry

3. Some Recollections of My Early Days in Carnyorth 1904-1923

as told by Charles Clifford Harry to his daughter Carlene Harry

Carlene Harry

I was born to Charles and Lillie Harry in 1904 at Wesley House, now Frimley House, in Carnyorth, a hamlet on the coast road between Lands End and St Ives, approximately two miles north of St Just. The house, formerly two miner's cottages, was part of the winnings of my maternal great-greatgrandfather and his brother in a poker game in the early 1800s, and was converted by my grandparents, Andrew and Mary Stevens, on their return from America in 1892.

I was named Charles on my birth certificate but realising that there were then three Charles Harrys living in Carnyorth (my father, grandfather and me), I was given the name Clifford as well on baptism and that is the name by which I was known.

Mining of tin and some copper had been the mainstay of the parish economy until the 1870s depression. By 1904 only one mine, Levant, was still working. Botallack reopened in 1906. The majority of miners at this time were working overseas, particularly in America, Australia and South Africa. Many had emigrated with their families, although some travelled to and fro.

My first memory is of the day of my greatgrandmother Mary Wall's funeral. She died when I was about 18 months old. I do not remember her but my mother told me I used to go next door to her cottage and talk to her. My sister and I were put to bed early. The light was shut out by dark curtains over the window and chairs were placed around the bed to keep us in. I tried to crawl out through the bars but became stuck. My screams brought my mother upstairs. Unable to comfort me she took me downstairs to where there were about eight old ladies wearing bonnets, black, fitting close to the head and tied under the chin, black blouses and thick black skirts, so long that they swept the floor.

Clifford House with Clifford's mother and grandmother at the door (Family Album)

Horsebus in Pendeen (Courtesy Morrab Library)

In those days a funeral was a major event and regrettably a frequent one. All close relatives went into deep mourning. This usually entailed a seven-mile horse-bus journey: two hours into Penzance and, as it was uphill, three hours back along very rough roads churned up by the large traction engines pulling trucks of coal from Penzance harbour. Unrelieved black was purchased as well as cotton gloves for the bearers, black if the deceased was an adult, white if a child. Hearses were unknown so on the day of the funeral there were eight or twelve bearers, two sets, who carried the coffin often up to two miles. In some cases where the stairs were awkward long planks were angled from the bedroom window so that the coffin could slowly slide down to the waiting bearers. Friends led the procession,

23

often with the church or a chapel choir singing hymns between them and the coffin which was followed by the relatives.

Levant Mine's Fowler road locamotive, pulling a train. These were usually loaded with coal or ore (Courtesy Morrab Library)

By the time I was about three years old, I felt the urge to explore the wider world; so discovering how to open the gates onto the road I ventured forth dressed in old clothes. A frantic search ensued and I was duly brought home, smacked hard and told I was a very naughty boy. To prevent a recurrence the two gates were tied together but I found I could squeeze between the bars and one Saturday afternoon, again dressed in my oldest clothes, I sallied forth and found my way to the field where Trewellard cricket team was playing. Once again I was found, taken home and suffered. By this time Mother felt drastic action had to be taken, as it was quite dangerous for a child of my age to be out on the road, particularly since, although there was no motor traffic in 1908, there was a hill with two sharp corners, one just above and one just below our gate around which horses often came at speed. Added to this was the shame it brought on respectable parents for their son to be seen by all the villagers wandering about uncared-for and unkempt. As a result, having explained to the head of Carnyorth Infants School what a worry I was and that I was reasonably intelligent and would like to go to school, the following week I was led there, in frock and pinafore, to start my education.

When we were quite young, Sundays followed a pattern. We put on clean underwear, and then with our best clothes on top we were dressed for chapel. Breakfast followed, after which we sat quietly and read or gave help where needed. Woe betides us if we made ourselves untidy! At about 10:15 we set off for the 10:30 service at Trewellard Wesleyan Chapel. After the service we returned home for midday dinner which was usually roast beef, potatoes and two other vegetables followed by a pudding. When everything was cleared away we went into the front room and read. Comic and weekly magazines were frowned on and story books were tolerated, but true Sunday reading was the Bible, Bible Stories, *Fox's Book of Martyrs* and my father's engagement present to my mother, *The Pilgrim's Progress* and *The Holy War*. Games were not played on Sundays, nor were cards. On other days we would play draughts, ludo, snakes and ladders and snap, but since playing cards were 'the devil's pasteboards' none were allowed into the house. At 2:15 we set off for Sunday school. On returning

Clifford in frock and petticoats with his sister Lilian c.1907 (Family album)

24

home we found a tea of bread and cream, sometimes jelly, apple or blackberry tarts and saffron cake, 'heavy' cake and buns (the results of Saturday's baking), awaiting us in the parlour, a room normally only used on a Sunday. At 5:45 we were off again to the evening service.

I was not always well behaved in chapel. I found it hard to sit still for long. If I was restless and fidgeted my mother would look at me. The next time she would lift a finger and if it happened a third time then I was caned on Monday. There was one time when I really behaved most reprehensively. I was seven, and at that age we were given no pocket money— just a few sweets and a few pence on high days and holidays. One Sunday I put my hand with its penny over the collection plate then withdrew it still holding the penny. I do not remember what occurred immediately, but my mother must have seen what happened as I had to write to my father in South Africa to confess my crime. On another occasion during a practice for recitation day several boys, including me, wandered into the vestry and, seeing the little wine-filled communion glasses, drank the contents.

A very vivid picture of what happened one Sunday morning when I was about eight is still with me. The service was proceeding as usual when, suddenly during the sermon, an old lady in heavy black gasped for breath and fell

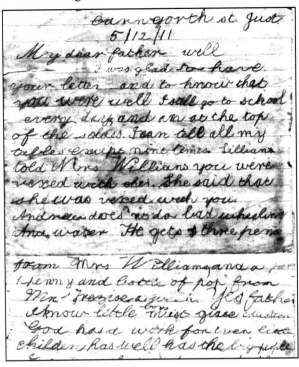

Letter from Clifford to his father confessing to retaining his chapel collection (Family papers)

forward in her pew. Men near by rushed to help her but it was too late. It was a fatal heart attack. As I sat watching I just kept thinking how wonderful it was to die in chapel during the service. She must surely go straight to heaven.

By the time I was in my late teens, the Sunday pattern changed. My friends and I did not always go to Sunday School but on fine days roamed the cliffs around Botallack mine. As we were wearing our best clothes we had to be circumspect and keep away from mine shafts and adits. We did, however, scramble up and down cliffs with some risk to life and limb. One Sunday as we were passing a building used by Camborne School of Mines there was a heavy shower. Noticing a large broken window we crawled through it, had a smoke and experimented with some of the chemicals. We did this several more times until the glass was replaced. The local policeman came to the Carnyorth School where I was a pupil teacher to seek information about the intruders. Fortunately none was forthcoming but we avoided Botallack cliffs for the next couple of months.

We then spread our wings in other directions. The largest chapel in our parish was at St Just so in the evenings my friends and I started to go there, because, I confess, of the greater choice of girls there. On fine summer evenings we walked along the cliffs to the service, a journey that took longer and longer until we did not arrive until chapel was over. This led to an awkward dilemma. My mother always asked me the text so I had to

Clifford with his mother, sister Lilian and brother Winston c. 1910 (Family album)

tread warily since if, during the following week, she met one of her St Just friends she was quite capable of saying 'Clifford tells me Mr…. took his text from …… and preached a very good sermon'. Fortunately I had a school friend in St Just who could not play truant, as his parents attended chapel, so he kindly noted the text, chapter and verse, and passed the information on to me. Instead of attending the service we might be found lying on the bank of the Nancherrow river trying to tickle trout or playing pitch-and-toss with our collection money. There was one occasion when I won the lot finishing in pocket by 2/-, no mean sum in those days. Associated with chapel were Tea Treats, where after tea various games were played such as Kiss in the Ring enjoyed by teenagers of both sexes.

Clifford with his mother, sister Lilian and brother Winston c. 1916 (Family album)

Monday was wash day. An iron container, with handles, was filled with water and put on the slab in the kitchen. The water was from the large rainwater barrel outside the back door, one of several around the outside of the house. In summer if we ran out of rainwater, water had to be brought from the communal well. The long wash tub, 4 feet long and 18 inches wide and deep, was brought into the back kitchen from the coal house and put on two trestles. Fel Naptha soap was used; the soaped article was then rubbed on a corrugated and perforated zinc scrubbing board, before finally being mangled between two heavy rollers. Care was needed when feeding the mangle as while turning the handle it was easy to squash one's fingers between the rollers. (This occasionally happened.) There was a passage between our house and the cottage next door where on wet days clothes were hung to dry against the house wall which was always warmed by the fire in the slab. We had two types of iron, flat and box. The former was placed on the slab to heat up and was spat on to test if it was hot enough for use. The latter had a solid piece of iron about 3x4 inches with a hole through its side which, when red hot and with the aid of a poker, could be placed in the iron through a side which moved up and down.

Saturday was baking day: saffron cake and buns, heavy and other sorts of cake, and bread for the following week were baked. Occasionally bread was bought from the baker in Pendeen. For me it was the day the knife-box full of knives, spoons and forks came out. The knife-board, rounded at one end, was sprinkled with knife powder and the cutlery was drawn over it, up and down, several times pressing hard against the board. When the cutlery was washed it shone. This was also the day we had our baths. Water was heated in a cast iron boiler on the slab, coconut matting placed on the floor and the bath placed on that. The boiler was large enough to give an ample supply of hot water so one could do more than just 'in, wash and out'. In winter a hot bath in a warm room was quite a luxury.

Personal cleanliness was important, and we were compelled to wash regularly. When we came down in the morning we washed immediately in cold water, even though in winter it often meant first breaking the ice in the barrel just outside the back door. Of course ladies had water up on the washstands and, if we had guests who stayed the night, hot water was carried up for them. That *was* a luxury.

There were other tasks that had to be done. The cement-surfaced kitchen floor had to be swept regularly. There were two methods of keeping any dust down, either dampened used tea-leaves, profusely scattered, or damp sand brought from the cove in a donkey cart. The floor was then swept and the tea leaves or sand thrown on the ash pile. Oil lamps and candles were the only means of lighting. When in use all the lamps underwent a daily inspection. First all traces of smoke were cleaned from the glasses and globes, then the wicks were turned up and trimmed, the oil wells filled and the bodywork cleaned and polished. All grease was removed from the candlesticks and the wicks pinched to get rid of any 'dead' cotton so that all was ready for the evening. In summer when numerous small red worms appeared out through their tap the rainwater barrels had to be vigorously scrubbed out with hot soapy water, rinsed and carefully wiped.

Clifford's maternal grandmother, Mary Stevens c. 1907 (Family album)

I had my own particular chores. I started fetching water from the communal well when I was quite young. Initially I had to stop three or four times to rest on the uphill journey of about 200 yards. When I first managed the journey without stopping, I felt I was really growing up. In summer the water-level sank and, if it was a dry September, it was so low that the bucket scraped along the bottom a few hours after the well had been in use. Then one went as early as possible because amongst other uses this water was our only source of drinking water. In winter the level rose, reaching a drain near the top from which it ran away in quite a stream. Our drinking water was stored in earthenware bussas (pots/jars). Other bussas held pilchards in brine, butter in brine and eggs in isinglass.

As I grew up my tasks increased. There was no man in the house as my father, Charles Harry, was in South Africa. One of my first regular tasks was to wheel away the ashes and rubbish to a corner of the garden. Later I was sent shopping, to a shop in Trewellard armed with a basket and list, staggering home with such items as tea, treacle, rice, cheese, a quarter-pound of boiled sweets (usually brandy balls or acid drops) and perhaps brawn, margarine and potatoes. We were well fed, being given a sustaining breakfast of porridge, eggs, fried potatoes and bacon. Dinner was chiefly meat—beef, pork or mutton, with potatoes and vegetables, followed by rice or tapioca pudding with plenty of milk; in the autumn, there might be some form of baked pudding, or blackberry or apple tart with Cornish cream. Tea saw a laden table, buttered bread with home-made jam or treacle and heavy, saffron or seed cake and in season we had tarts with cream. Special treats were jellies, tinned fruit, salmon and richer-than-usual cake. Supper was usually hot milk with arrowroot, or Horlicks or occasionally a mug of Bovril. One of my grandmother's maxims was 'feed them while they are young; if you don't it will be too late when they are 16 or 17.'

There were also boots and shoes to clean, the latter not worn by men or children. This was done on newspaper, on two granite steps by the back door. The kindling box had to be kept full. Boxes from the shop and odd pieces of wood from the mine were split on these same steps. Here, too, the hatchet was used to crack the bones of bony beef. On one occasion my maternal grandmother, who lived with us and did all the cooking, did this, striking the beef several hefty blows only to find that her spectacles being underneath were now twisted and shattered!

We kept fowls and in late summer I was sent out with a fern hook to cut bracken for their bedding. Once they stopped laying they were destined for the table and it was my job to decapitate them with a hatchet while someone held them firmly over a wooden block or to slit their weasands (throats) with a sharp knife. Once a week I had the exquisite job of emptying the two buckets from the privy.

Once our chores were done, we boys were free to run wild. In our early teens we felt immortal. This feeling led us to what I now realise were foolhardy exploits, some of which we were lucky to survive. There were many unused but still accessible mine shafts. Of these Nineveh still had sound ladders which we discovered. When I was about fourteen, six or so of us went down this shaft, about 20 fathoms to the first level where the shaft's continuation down was boarded over. With candles and torch we explored until one of the boys stepped on a plank which was just balanced on a cross beam, so that the end he stepped on went down. Fortunately he was able to grasp an upright beam and step off onto another plank. We were all very scared and climbed to the surface without further exploration.

All disused shafts were walled to prevent animals and even humans meeting an untimely end, but there were many adits in the side of the cliff. We went through these dark forbidding tunnels, their roofs supported by half-rotten pit props, a continuous stream at our feet and, at intervals, little piles of rubbish where the roof had caved in: but what we feared most was the slime. Where the roof was low it might easily rub off on to our jackets and, if this was seen when we got home, our parents would realise our foolhardiness and it meant a real thrashing.

The rugged cliffs had many inlets usually with tortuous paths leading down to the shore or to rocks a few feet above the shore, and these were our hunting ground. The rocks could be dangerous when an unusually high wave unexpectedly swept shoreward. One inlet immediately below Botallack mine had first a path, then a ladder still in a reasonable state of preservation. Below this was a very narrow cleft only a few yards deep across the top of which a beam had been placed and a stout rope attached to it. As we could always touch the sides and there was really no danger, we often went there to see if any wreck timbers had been washed in or to have a quiet smoke. Even in my young days boys smoked. We were too young to buy cigarettes so we found substitutes. The favourite was 'drain crane' cut into cigarette sized pieces. Others were made of certain dried leaves and mosses known as 'roadside' mixture but this was not as popular.

At Avarack several pools of various depths were left at ebb tide. In the more shallow pools we floundered until as we grew older we ventured into the deeper ones where we learnt to swim. Usually we took our first dip at Easter and carried on until late August. The water coming in from the Atlantic was usually quite cool so each swim was of comparatively short duration. As we grew older we swam in the sea, usually at Portheras Cove. There was a narrow inlet at the northern extremity of Avarack known as Pulbean. It was about ten yards wide and to us quite deep, but as soon as we felt confident enough we swam across it and back. We then thought we had no need to worry if we ever found ourselves out of our depth in water.

Carnyorth Moor, the unclaimed land in front of Long Row and the main road, little travelled after working hours, all lent themselves to various games and activities. As we could hear a car or horse even before we could see what was coming it was safe to play on the road. As infants we played 'horses'. A longish cord was tied around each arm of the horse and used as reins by the driver. As wages were low there was no money for toys or any but the cheapest of materials—indeed much of what we used in games and activities was homemade. We bought wooden tops and marbles, but kites were made at home and iron hoops were made in the blacksmith's shop. The hoops we drilled for many a mile. Such exercise was especially invigorating on a frosty moonlit night. There were two models of kite: square toppers, easier to make, and round toppers made from lathes of wood, string, paper, often newspaper, and a flour paste, all easily obtainable materials.

Sometimes on dry nights two boys would wander off to play *Knick-Knock*. Many cottages had no front gardens so they would cautiously go to a window, push a stout pin into the wood and over this place a piece of thin string or cotton with a very small stone attached. Pulling and then loosening the string made the stone rattle against the glass often making someone in the house come out. At the sound of movement the perpetrators glided quickly away melting into the darkness—it must be remembered there was no form of street lighting. There was however the risk that people inside guessed what was happening. On one occasion two friends of mine were string-pulling when an upstairs window opened and from it descended the contents of a water bucket. A variation of this was the glass-bottle-and-gravel method. One threw a handful of large gravel against the window while the other simultaneously dashed the bottle against the wall of the house and then fled. Here again the method was not foolproof. On one occasion the man of the house came to the door and, although the miscreants had fled, unfortunately one stumbled and hit the other and they both fell into the nettles where they had to stay until the man re-entered the cottage. There was another method of annoyance caused by our activities. The doors of the cottages had outside handles rather than knobs so with good stout cord we would tie two adjacent handles together and then knock on both doors. If there was no back door, efforts to open the front one became frantic; on some occasions one of our number having been left near the cottages while we retreated well away, waited for a lull when he could untie the cord and if possible creep silently away. This was not always simple as we all wore hobnail boots which on contact with the metal surface of the road betrayed our whereabouts. Another pastime was un-hanging garden gates, taking them some distance away and depositing them in a farmer's field, but this only happened on a certain night each year—I forget which.

Donkeys, too, did not escape our attention. On Carn Kenidjack there were usually several of them spanned (hobbled) or tethered finding a precarious existence. These were used by their owners as transport to the mines where they worked. The animal was harnessed to a crude conveyance comprising shafts and two wheels with a plank across on which the miner sat with his feet almost touching the ground. Now these donkeys constituted a challenge. Taking advantage of moonlit nights we would go to the Carn and catch one and then try to ride it. There were three possible results. The first was a quiet but unexciting ride on an amenable donkey; the second on a lively moke which twisted, turned and bucked, quite often unseating its jockey; the third on a recalcitrant beast which would not move. If we tried to pull it along, it dug in its front hooves and there was an impasse. Similarly if we pushed it, it kept its heels firm, so it was stalemate. Not to be outdone we had recourse to sterner methods. We did not agree with too much physical kindness, and we knew from experience both at home and at school that physical pain often produced results, so one of us cut a useful gorse twig which, having first taken a strategic position to avoid any plunging hooves, he applied to a tender part of the obstinate animal's hind quarters. Usually the result was electric—a violent plunge forward. Usually, too, the jockey hung on like grim death, arms tightly and 'lovingly' round the animal's neck, knees pressed firmly into its sides. Old hands managed to hold on but tyros sometimes were not successful, but these unfortunates always seemed to be intelligent and agile enough to fall clear of any of those plunging hooves but not necessarily of a patch of gorse.

Penzance County Grammar School VI Form 1921, Clifford back row on right (Family album)

Naturally we had a number of 'acceptable' games which we played on the waste ground adjoining the school. The favourite was marbles usually played 'for good' that is if we won a marble we kept it.

Not for us, however, the mechanical throwing of a marble along a gutter trying to hit the preceding one. We preferred something more skilful. We had three variations: *Towns, Rings* or *Knuckle Pits*. On warmer days we played a more static game, *Five Stones*. Another activity was *Buck-sh-buck*, a form of leapfrog involving two teams of four or five. A 'pillow,' probably the smallest or least robust member of one team, stood against a wall while the others members lined up behind bent over with flat backs holding on to the one in front of them. The members of the other team ran up and vaulted on to the backs trying to get as close to the 'pillow' as possible. If a member of the 'receiving' team buckled under the weight of a vaulter, all those who had all ready jumped could go back and start again; but if they slid off or there was no space left on the backs for the last of the team, the teams reversed roles. If all the team were successfully astride and steady the pillow held one of his hands out of sight to all but an umpire and extended a number of fingers saying 'How many?' If the opponents gave the wrong number, then the teams reversed their roles. We played two forms of hide-and-seek, *Kick the Bucket*, on the rough ground in front of Long Row, using former piggeries, hedges, walls, etc., as hiding places. An empty Tate & Lyle Golden Syrup tin was the 'bucket' where the seeker stood to count and those hiding tried to run to and kick the tin away without being caught. *Guarding the Flag* was played on Carnyorth Moor which gave a much larger area for hiding. A Union Jack on a pole was placed atop one of the many banks to be guarded by the seeker. A narrow block of granite protruding from a wall by about a foot was used to play *Duck*. Each boy found a piece of granite roughly the size of a brick. One player, the guardian, put his on top of the block then stood a little way to the side. The others lined up about twelve to fifteen feet away and in turn threw their stones, attempting to dislodge the target. If the target was hit the guardian replaced it as quickly as possible while the others picked up their stones and ran back to the throwing point. Should the stone be replaced and one of these be caught and touched, before he reached safety he became guardian. If all threw without dislodging the target they had to pick up their stones and run back. Usually the guardian caught and touched one who then became the new guardian.

Swedes, known to us as turnips, were grown for cattle feed. On moonlit evenings we lifted—in both senses of the word—some of these turnips, one between two, cut each in half, then scooped out the flesh having half a turnip each. We nearly all had knives. We ate the flesh leaving an inch of thickness all over. Into this we stuck a wooden skewer like piece of wood which was used as a mast holding a paper sail. In winter there were several pools on the moor so we raced our ships over these. Usually there was at least a reasonable breeze.

It was seldom extremely cold, but when we did get some ice we slid along it. Since it rarely froze hard, often one of us fell through it. Still none of the pools was very deep so we all survived albeit slinking home at times wet and miserable and fearful of retribution if unable to get upstairs unseen. As frosts were rare, we made slides on banks on the moor, pouring water on a six-inch line then sliding down. The trouble there was that our muddied boots had to be cleaned, given a spit and polish, before going to school next morning First we moistened the upper, then put blacking on, finally brushing to give a shine which could sometimes take ten minutes to achieve.

Shrove Tuesday was known as *Tubbing Day*. A Tubbin, a piece of turf, was dug up from a waste patch with a hob-nailed boot. When we were all armed, we divided into two sides several yards from each other and threw turfs while dodging any that came in our direction.

Football was played on the road in the moonlight. The ball often consisted of a few sizeable rags lightly tied with string or a Tate & Lyle's 2lb treacle tin. As we wore hob-nailed boots our shins often suffered. Sometimes we played football and cricket with boys from neighbouring hamlets, but these games, regrettably, often ended in arguments (we had no referees or umpires) and stone fights. There were plenty of roughly egg-sized stones lying about. I do not remember anyone being really hurt, so perhaps it was not as bad as it sounds.

A relic of the 'hungry' days, in which I did not take part, were the bird traps which many boys set regularly with varied success. On nights when the foliage was thin they went bush-beating, three or four in a group, each with a stout stick and torch. Any unfortunate bird caught in the torch's beam was quickly dispatched. On rare occasions sparrows were caught and 'baked in a pie'.

I did not regret, indeed I did not realise, that in many ways we lived a primitive existence: no water laid on, no rubbish collections and no flush toilets, as our freedom to roam made life wonderful.

4. Goldsithney School

Joan Howells

At the opening of the Perranuthnoe School Board school on Monday, the children were entertained with tea and buns which were provided out of subscriptions received from the chairman Mr J Laity and Mrs Trevelyan. The old Association Methodist Chapel and two cottages adjoining with about a quarter of an acre of land, under the skilful direction and superintendence of Mr John Trounson, architect, Penzance, has been economically converted into a convenient school and premises at a cost of nearly £200. Mr George Harris, mason of Marazion and Messrs TJ Leggo, carpenters, Madron, have satisfactorily carried out their respective contracts. Messrs Holman and sons supplied the desks. The mistress, late of Guernsey, is Miss Lanyon, a native of Helston. The school will accommodate 140 girls and infants.[51]

Goldsithney School, 2007

This account of the opening of Goldsithney School started our research into the history of one of the many village elementary schools that closed during the twentieth century. Prior to 1876, when the government made elementary education compulsory, the children who had an education were taught at Dame schools or Sunday schools.

In 1840 Lady Carrington, the lady of the manor of Trevelyan, Perranuthnoe, had a private school built to accommodate 75 boys and 75 girls in separate schoolrooms, with fees from 1½d to 3d a week. Thirty years later this school was transferred to the parish as a Church of England school for boys only. It was therefore necessary for girls and infants to be educated elsewhere and the redundant Wesley Methodist Association chapel, built in 1841, was chosen as the most suitable building. The conversion was finished in 1879, keeping the attractive old Gothic-style chapel windows so that the two large rooms (each 30' x 20') overlooked South Street. Fifty-nine children were enrolled on the first day and the early weeks saw this increase to 70.

From these first days to the last, a requirement of this and every school was that the head-teacher should keep a log-book. This was a bare record of the events that constitute the history of the school and 'no opinions or reflections were to be entered'. Through these four log-books,[52] kept over nine decades, the details and highlights of life in the area retain a vivid reality. School Boards, elected by male and female ratepayers, were created to control fundraising and organisation. Attendance officers

---

[51] The *Cornishman*, 17 July 1879.
[52] Goldsithney School Log Books

were appointed for weekly inspection of the attendance books and they had the authority to report parents to the magistrates should their children be absent with no valid reason or doctor's certificate. It was essential that the level of attendance should be high, because the grants from the Board on which the school depended would be affected by poor turnout. It appears that in the early days the Board had considerable difficulty in appointing headmistresses: by 1883 no fewer than four teachers had held the post. Consequently the inspector commented that 'work has been carried out under great disadvantage but the progress of the scholars was not unsatisfactory. They read well, write fairly and have made some progress in arithmetic'. However, one cannot help but be intrigued when learning that 'the younger children are unable to perform the complex calculations without mechanical aid'.

In the first year it is apparent that some local traditions had precedence over school attendance. The biggest event of the Goldsithney calendar was the Feast of St James on 5 August. Despite the members of the Board giving a whole day's holiday 'the attendance this week was very small owing to the Fair'. St Piran's Day on 5 March was celebrated in the same way and, as 'only six children presented themselves, a whole holiday instead of the afternoon was given'. The Board allowed several holidays throughout the year for Cornish tea treats, fairs, the Royal Cornwall show, etc., and of course this agricultural district allowed longer breaks for potato and corn harvesting. On 7 April 1902 the King's yacht arrived at Mount's Bay and the school closed for the afternoon 'in order that all might have an opportunity of seeing the King who landed at Marazion'.

Goldsithney Fair, c. 1900 The Feast of St James

Contagious diseases were widespread and several deaths were recorded from measles, scarlet fever and whooping cough. By comparison, in 1880, Sarah Mollard was fortunate to only faint for 45 minutes! Another major factor for absenteeism was the weather. During the winter months the roads were almost impassable and the lanes around Goldsithney were sometimes quagmires due to horse-drawn traffic and the movement of cattle. The children had to walk to school and, as some ex-pupils recall, the schoolroom stove was often surrounded by drying shoes and stockings.

With an average attendance of 100 it was found difficult to cope with just two rooms, and a third classroom was built in 1900. The inspector now commented, 'the new classroom is a great boon and [the school] will in future proceed under more favourable conditions'. After the Balfour Act of 1902 the School Boards were abolished and the school became known as Perranuthnoe Elementary School for boys and girls up to the age of twelve, but many stayed for a further one or two years.

Lessons started with religious instruction and hymn-singing. Poetry too played a large part and poems such as 'The Lady of the Lake' and 'The Wreck of the Hesperus' had to be learned by heart. The boys concentrated on arithmetic and geography, with the girls being taught 'domestic economy, plain darning and feather stitching'. Our oldest ex-pupil, Doris Day née Laity (at the time of writing still living in Goldsithney at the age of 101) can recall making a chemise at school for which the girls had to supply the calico. Clay modelling was one of the more creative subjects taught and nature walks were included in the school agenda, with as many as fifty different wild flowers being recorded during one particular outing. Twelve-year-olds were required to study 'calculations based on the prices and analysis of artificial manures'—a discipline unlikely to find a place in today's curriculum.

The log-books give little indication of the impact made on the children of Goldsithney by the First World War. Isabel Berriman remembered leaving the school at the very start of the war and finding the wide Fore Street lined with horses: the Government had ordered all sound horses owned by local farmers to be brought to Goldsithney so that those suitable could be commandeered by the Army. This start to the war saddened a community for whom horses were a means of transport, companions and an economic necessity. At the end of that

Fore Street, Goldsithney c. 1910

appalling war in 1918 a disastrous influenza outbreak swept through Europe. A local tragedy was the death of Mrs Laity of Trevabyn who died leaving six children, three of whom were attending Goldsithney School. Father Bernard Walke in *Twenty Years at St Hilary* writes about the shocked reaction to her sudden death and about the devastating effect of the 'flu on the two parishes. 'There were six funerals in the first week of the epidemic', and he and Annie Walke his wife accommodated children from stricken families in 'The Jolly Tinners' and the St Hilary Vicarage. An extra week's holiday was given in the summer of 1919 to celebrate the signing of the peace and Remembrance Day became established in the school calendar.

After 1918, there was a steady decline in numbers, mainly due to emigration. In 1923 the school became an infant school only, with both boys and girls aged five to seven. This meant that the average attendance fluctuated between twelve and twenty, and only one schoolroom was used.

Within the school community much depended on the Headmistress. The first head was Miss Lanyon and she was followed by thirteen other headmistresses over ninety years. The inspector's report gives a glowing report of the pupils' conduct and achievements under Miss Furse. She was followed by Miss Mitchell, and in 1930 the popular Miss Edmonds came from St Hilary School to take up duties as Headmistress for the next 25 years. Many in the district today remember Miss Edmonds as a friend as well as a teacher who made early school days so enjoyable. One ex-pupil says, 'My mother used to send me with cheese sandwiches which I did not like—I used to cry. Miss Edmonds would cover them in HP sauce so that I would eat them—that's the sort of kind person she was.'

Head Mistresses	
1879	Miss Lanyon
1883	Miss Roach
1883	Miss Andrews (assistant)
1883	Miss Goodall
1883	Miss Bradbury
1884	Miss Everinghome
1885	Miss Thomas
1886	Miss Penrose
1891	Miss Thomas
1909	Miss Coulis
1923	Miss Furse
1927	Miss Mitchell
1930	Miss Edmonds
1955	Miss Mayes
1969	Closed

It took almost fifty years after 1879 for the authorities to show concern for the children's health. The inspector in 1907 considered both schoolrooms to be insufficiently heated at 51 degrees; in November of that year one child died of pneumonia. Medical inspections started in 1909 when 27 children were weighed and measured. In later years this was undertaken by another local figure—Dr Chown. Nurse Miners, the district nurse, made regular cleanliness inspections, and the first dental check was in 1939.

Drinking water from the school tank was deemed unsafe, and even that from the public stand had to be boiled, and it was not until 1956 that mains water was installed. The lavatories—referred to as 'the offices'—were initially earth closets, and it was not until 1955 that flush lavatories were introduced. All whitewashed and scrubbed by the indispensable Mrs Rowe, they were 'a great joy and advantage to the school'. The playground was enlarged, the water-tank removed and the schoolroom painted.

During the World War II, the school was designated a reception area for evacuees. As elsewhere, windows had to be taped or shuttered, fuel was in short supply and gas-masks had to be worn for ten minutes each day, even on nature walks. The Home Guard used the large schoolroom for lectures, fire-drill and gas training. There was also a cinema show given by the Ministry of Information to inform teachers and children of the procedure in case of invasion. The church bells, that of Acton Castle and the school bell were to be rung for at least ten minutes. However, by 1944, the evacuees had returned home, and then on 8 May the following year, victory in Europe meant a three-day holiday.

Miss Hayes with the class of 1950

Miss Edmonds left in 1955 and Miss Mayes took on the headship. She had many new ideas, the first being a sports day which became a regular feature, together with Christmas parties where 'the children brought lovely food. The tea and pop was provided out of school funds, also the four jellies'.

From being 'unruly and ignorant' in the first year of operation, in the nineteenth century, the pupils became 'very neat and orderly' and produced 'written exercises which are worthy of praise'. Later, with Miss Edmonds, the report states that 'she enjoys the complete confidence of her pupils and provides them with a happy introduction to school life…It is particularly satisfying to record the independence shown by the children and the natural way they go about their work.' For well over half of the twentieth century this school had been the cornerstone of village life, and through two world wars, unemployment and economic depression it remained a stable and happy environment. Unfortunately with the steady decline in numbers and improvements in transport, it became apparent that another of our village schools would have to close. We end with the last and rather sad entry in the fourth log-book:

The Christmas decorations have come down for the last time after ninety years. The little school is closing for good and the children going to St Hilary or Marazion. Miss Mayes is retiring after thirteen years, training and teaching little people five to seven years old. She wishes them well and hopes the seeds she has sown will materialise well. Nearly all the equipment is going to St Hilary School.[53]

---

[53] Goldsithney School Log Book No 4, 19 Dec 1969

5. Zennor Farmers, Some Old Codgers

Jean Nankervis

Introduction

Much has been written about farming in the first half of the 20th century so I have concentrated on the second half. For Zennor we are lucky to have *Tremedda Days* by Alison Symons which expertly covers 1900-1944. An excellent supplement to this is *The Changing Farm 1900-1980* by Zennor WI.[54]

Zennor is a parish on the north Cornish coast fourteen miles from Land's End and two miles west of St Ives. It is about four miles long and one mile deep. The fields are small and strewn with granite boulders. Their Cornish hedges are built of rocks and earth and colonised by a variety of wildlife. Those built in the Bronze Age are among the oldest man-made features in the world still used for the purpose for which they were made. The farms stretch out along the plateau above the 100 metre high cliffs which are pounded incessantly by the Atlantic. To the south the land rises to the open downs where livestock roamed freely a hundred years ago. In 1987 Zennor and the surrounding countryside was designated an Environmentally Sensitive Area. We must keep the hedges in good repair and not enlarge our tiny fields. The boulders that make work in the fields so difficult have been photographed from the air and may not be moved.

There is a small settlement around the church of ten houses, not all lived in full time, a pub, a hostel and the Wayside Museum. About a mile to the west is The Gurnard's Head Hotel with its public bar.

In 1960 when I came to Zennor there were 28 dairy farms. The milk-stand for churns at the top of each lane was used by one or more farmers. Every farmer was a Zennor man or one of his relations, except at Trendrine. Now, in the year 2006, there is half that number of farmers because many have taken over neighbouring land. However, the same families run all but two of the farms.

Figure 1 On Christmas Day ten sat down to dinner at Wicca

The electoral roll has increased from about 135 in 1960 to 173 in 2000 of which 50 are now concerned with farming. A variety of people live in the farming hamlets and occupations include teacher, artist, writer, priest, publisher, bar staff, architect, computer programmer, National Trust warden, secretary and retired residents.

Some of the farmers in this article may be called Old Codgers and the most senior of these is John Loosemore. He lived at the eastern end of Zennor parish at Trevail. On the other side of the river, in Towednack parish, his grandfather, Arthur Hollow, farmed Trevega Wartha. In 1912 Arthur Hollow arranged for his daughter Isabel to live at Trevail Mill, on the Zennor side, with his mother and his sister (known as Aunt Elizabeth). His eldest daughter, Sarah, married Sam Nankervis in 1909, and another daughter, Janey, wed Leonard Berryman, also a Zennor farmer. Isabel wed Ernest Loosemore and John was born in 1921. Sarah and Sam Nankervis had seven children including my husband Gordon. Four of the seven farmed in Zennor and the youngest, Jenny, married Henry Semmens (see page 37) and they ran Aunt Janey's farm at Boswednack (see pull-out map).

Trevail and Trendrine are the most easterly farms in Zennor and on their western boundaries are Wicca and Boscubben. Trendrine has its own lane from the main road but the second farm lane leads to Boscubben, Wicca and Trevail. On the other side of Zennor Churchtown is Trewey where Sam Nankervis had one of the three farms until his family moved to Wicca in 1931. In 1945 Arthur Mann's family came to Trewey and had the other two farms.

---

[54] For full bibliographical information on all references, see the Bibliography on pp. 113-116

35

John Loosemore has retired to Sennen and now I run Wicca with my daughter Rose. The other Old Codgers in this article are Arthur Mann and his wife Nora. They were married in 1950 and still live at Trewey where their son Harry and his family run the farm.

John Loosemore's Account[55]

I was born in Trevail Mill in 1921, the most northerly house in the parish. My father was 48 when I was born. He was brought up in London and was trained as an electrician by Compton Electrical Engineers. He worked on the Underground for a while. Later he became a motor engineer and worked for Lord Cowdray as a chauffeur. By 1909 he had an international driving license with his picture on and all. I've still got it. There are very few about. My father came here to put electricity into Giew Mine [at Cripplesease] and then he met mother, about 1919 I suppose, and went on from there. He didn't know anything about farming but Grandfather [Hollow], who farmed Trevega Wartha, asked the Porthia Estate [his landlord] if they [John's parents] could have his bit of land beyond the mill. We kept a few cows and always had pigs. It formed a separate holding and we just had that twelve acres till we rented Higher Trevail Farm in 1945.

Figure 2 John and Marjorie Loosemore, 2003

For some reason my father sent me to St Ives School. I was 5½ years old and it was a 3½ mile walk up through Trevega and Trevalgan. I didn't pick up anyone to go with until I passed through there. There was an old chapel then in Trevalgan Lane. Coming home I'd sometimes walk up the Stennack with the old chap who used to light the gas lamps all the way up to Consols; still had 2½ mile to go. I'd go down Bal Lane from Trevega Wartha to our house. You could drive a car down there then, it's only a path now. Later I had a bike. When Zennor School closed in 1935 they all came down to St Ives on a bus, so I could too. I walked up the lane to Wicca to catch the bus. Before that we always went Trevega way to St Ives, saved a mile at least. I went to church a bit. I'd go with the Nankervises from Wicca when they moved there in 1930s. They were bell ringers and Gordon was the organist.

My mother's Aunt Elizabeth lived with my mother at Trevail when she went down there in 1912. She was born in 1839 and died aged 105 in 1943. I grew up with her living in our house. She remembered going as a small child with *her* grandmother, who must have been born in the eighteenth century, to collect money to build the Bible Christian Chapel by Wicca river. It's been a ruin for years. Aunt Elizabeth's mother, my great grandmother, died at Trevail in 1919 aged 100. Her father lived to 97. They're all three in that grave just inside the churchyard, average age 100.

My mother started in the visitor trade in 1924. It kept them going through the Great Depression and all when farming went down. She'd built up the trade till we had up to a dozen people there. I know they only paid 25 to 30 bob [shillings, £1.50] a week, but you thought you were doing well. In the '30s when me and Willy [Craze] was growing up as boys we used to keep our mothers going with rabbits. Willy lived at Lower Trevega and is two years older than me. Willy's mum took in visitors too. We'd go out with our guns every night: the visitors would eat rabbit, all cheap, going to help out. We had a .410 poacher's gun. You could fold it in half and put it in your pocket. You'd shoot one, gut it there and then: if you wasn't happy with what was inside you'd dump it and shoot another. Must have shot hundreds, thousands all round Trevalgan cliff and all. When you got home you cut the head off, skinned it and cut it in four parts and put it in an enamel bowl of salted water overnight. Well, I can see the younger generation doing that today—eh?

[55] Some of this information is from an interview which appeared in *The Mermaid's Echo*. My thanks go to Chunky Penhaul for his help and for allowing me to use it.

Then came the Second World War. Willy pulled a wooden hut up top of Trendrine Hill with a horse and wagon so us Home Guard could settle in at night. No one lived in Carn Cottage on Zennor Hill so we used that too. Me and Willy watched a string of small bombs coming across from Heather Brea: they stopped at the back of Foage luckily. You had three shifts up there at night. One morning the last shift came off duty at 6 and didn't wake up the rest of them, left them up there. We all played tricks on each other then.

Marjorie, my wife, arrived from London. She first came on holiday in 1930. She was a visitor; I've known her 75 years. We were married in 1944 and took over Trevail Farm in 1945. She took on the whole package, working with horses when we started. I've got a picture of her in a field behind a roller in bare feet! Trevail wasn't a bad corn farm really. We used to have a couple of days threshing every year. All the inland side of the farm is granite but the cliff side hasn't got a granite rock in it, all blue elvan and greenstone. We spent 40 years there. We did make a farm of it: it was a poor farm when we went in—red with sorrel due to lack of manure and lime. Jamie Osborne farmed Trevail before us and his advice was never to keep more than 24 cattle on it: when I left I had 187.

Before the Osbornes the Semmens were at Higher Trevail—when I was growing up in the '20s— Henry Semmens and his brothers and sister. There was an adit [drainage tunnel] which went in behind the mill, under the field called the Cattans, and on under our farm house at Higher Trevail. When old Mrs Semmens lived there she said she could hear the men working underneath the kitchen when the mine was working. In the 1976 drought you could see the snow-white lines across the garden and all up through the fields to Wicca. The ordinary grass had dried out and there were white lines where the adits were underneath. The same seam of tin ran all the way from Trevega Bal [mine], through Trevail and up to Wicca.

We were forced to grow broccoli and potatoes in the war years and we went on with that for a few years after. I grew a lot of kale, all different sorts, and flat-pole cabbage and mangolds, all for fodder. I used to work with Willy Craze a bit. He married two months before me and was living at Chykembro. We'd plant cabbages together. His tractor caught fire out here once, one of the little grey Fergies. You had to keep the rain off the magneto in those days and fiddle with spark plugs to stop them sooting up. We put up some huge gate posts together. His tractor got lifted off the ground doing one lot; didn't have the big machinery then.

We started milking by hand, then machine, then pipeline so we progressed along the road but we couldn't carry on when bulk tanks came in [1976]. The tankers couldn't get down the lane and it would have cost a fortune to widen it. It worked extremely well when we went over to beef. My neighbour, Dick Pengelly, he followed me. He came to Lower Trevega in 1950 and gradually took over all three farms there. We had a combining and contracting business together. The first combine we had came from over St Buryan way. We tried it out around the farmyard. Dick said 'How are we going to get it home with no license or insurance?' I said 'I'll drive it down through Penzance—no one will challenge you if you go that way.' So I did! Sailed along down through the town! They'd have stopped you on the back roads.

Heath and gorse fires don't do much damage if they move fast: the beauty of it is it gives plants a chance to grow. People don't realize that. You can see lots of things too in February/March just before the spring because the bracken's at its lowest. You can see all the old tracks and quillets [little meadows]. It's like that old saying,

Figure 3 The downs on fire above Wicca on 23 April 1997

'Live like you're going to die tomorrow, but farm like you're going to farm for ever.'

One of our favourite walks now is up Zennor Hill from Eagle's Nest. I had my mobile phone and I thought I'd ring our son Colin in Australia and tell him where his mother was. We had a bit of chat and he spoke to Marjorie and then I said, 'I'll tell you something nobody in Australia knows'. 'What's that?' 'The 4 o'clock bus is just leaving Zennor for St Ives!'

My Memories (Jean Nankervis)

I was married in 1960 when my husband Gordon farmed Wicca with his elder brother Arthur Nankervis. Their mother was Sarah Hollow, sister to John Loosemore's mother Isabel. My parents spent their honeymoon here and we came back for holidays. Like Marjorie, I trained as a teacher.

At Wicca I was responsible for 200 hens and the egg-money supplemented my housekeeping of £5 a week. The £5 fed me, Gordon and Arthur. Three children quickly arrived and I can remember working out that £5 meant I spent 1/- (5p) per person per meal. A fourth child was born in 1968 giving me two girls and two boys.

Figure 4 Jean in lane with George the dog, summer 1999

Every morning I went up the barn steps and filled an old enamel bowl three times with layers pellets. They had seven scoops of layers and one scoop of flake maize to make the yolks yellower. This was scattered on the hard ground, not in the mud, while I called, 'Cheepy, cheepy.' In the afternoon, while they were off their nests and feeding, I took an old basket with some hay in the bottom and picked up the eggs. When the hens were in full lay this was done in the morning as well. The hens laid all over the place. They had old orange boxes in their two houses, as well as little holes in the walls, under the haystacks, in the hedges; you had to know all the places and put a clome (china) egg in the empty nest when you picked up the eggs. If you left a nest empty the hen would make another one where you couldn't find it. They were fed approximately an hour before sunset all the year round. They went to roost at sunset before the foxes were about. I've seen a fox in the field circling the flock at midday and pick off a hen to feed cubs. I learnt all this from Gordon's Aunt Annie who was living here for the first year. She would see a hen coming in from the fields and then follow her next day to find where she was laying. Sometimes we found a nest full of eggs and brought them in to see if they floated in water. If they did we had to throw them away. Never leave egg shells about outside as they will give the dogs, crows and wildlife a taste for eggs. Aunt Annie looked rather like a hen herself with her beaked nose and bent back as she scurried after a cackling hen to find her nest.

In the evening about six dozen eggs were cleaned if necessary, and put on trays of 2½ dozen. These went into the big wooden egg box that held 30 dozen. I felt it was a real achievement when I needed a second box from March to June. My egg money varied each week from over £7 to under £1 depending on the time of year. In 1962 my profit for the year was £36/2/3d.

In the autumn I ordered 100 day old chicks for £16 which arrived from up-country by train. I collected the two boxes at St Erth. Each one had its beak dipped in water and when it shook its head we knew it was OK. They were kept warm with paraffin lamps until we had electricity put in. They were fed on meal and then baby chick crumbs. This meant the pullets came into lay in the spring. As they went off lay old hens had their heads chopped off. In 1961 I killed forty just in June and July. Then I would pluck them, open them and dress them. The Tinner's Arms made them into chicken pies. My first encounter with Gordon was sitting on the barn steps plucking hens for Aunt Annie to draw. Then we would go down together in his Landrover to deliver them.

Gordon and Arthur milked about 24 Guernsey cows. Each morning the churns were taken to the top of the lane for the milk lorry to collect. The milk cheque came in every month but it wasn't enough to keep us in the black. I took in visitors for bed and breakfast in the 1960s but then things changed in 1971 when Gordon's brother Arthur died. We put new stairs and floors in the cottage and let that out as well as two caravans. As soon as the four children were all old enough to go to school I did part-time teaching in local schools. When bulk milk tanks came in we went over to beef and by 1979 half the farmers in Zennor were in beef.[56] There are not many farm lanes a milk tanker can get down and now we only have four dairy herds in the parish.

In 1945, like everyone else, John Loosemore had Guernseys and milked by hand. Friesian cows give twice as much milk so, with the help of a milking machine he changed over in 1952. We stayed with Guernseys and got a premium for the higher butter fat. I asked John more about those days.

Conversation between John and Jean (me)

John said, 'Uncle Sam [Gordon's father] said it could never be done as Friesian cattle were too big for the small Zennor fields and the pasture wouldn't maintain them. I was getting the farm on its feet. Made 200 bales of hay to the acre.'

'Those were ½ cwt bales of hay, weren't they? The big round bales of silage we have today are nearly half a ton, that's twenty small ones. And Heston bales are even bigger.'

'Grasses are much faster growing now,' he said. 'They're much improved, especially the Cocksfoot. The old Cocksfoot was very rough and coarse, like the wild stuff growing down your cliff. Farmers are putting on more fertilizer, too. When I started at Higher Trevail in 1945 I took all our cows up there, about 12-14, I suppose. I bought in some heifers and a Guernsey bull. He was called Maurice and quite quiet, but when I had a Friesian bull he was savage so I went over to AI [artificial insemination]. We went up to 35-40 milkers and I made another six stalls when the pipeline was put in. Gordon never had a pipeline, did he?'

Figure 5 Unloading half-ton straw Heston bales in 1993. The tractor would tip forward if Rose drove down into the mowey so she has to reverse

'No, Gordon always had buckets,' I said, 'and when they were full they were too heavy for me to carry to the milk-house for cooling.'

'Friesians milked 6-8 gallons a day, that's a bucketful at every milking.'

'Guernseys milked four gallons but as they dried off Gordon could get two cows in a bucket.' (By 'two cows in a bucket' I mean the milk from two cows!)

'I calved all the year round,' he continued, 'and in summer I took up as many as 16 churns. The weight in the transport box on the back of the tractor was so great I had to back up the lane; the last bit, where it's so steep. I put my daughter Judy on the front once to weight it down but she wasn't heavy enough and got thrown into the green tree on the Boscubben bend. Your Gordon had 6-8 churns in the summer and we could hardly get them all on the milk stand. I suppose Boscubben sent up two for the morning and two for the afternoon.'

I said, 'Most people had more milk in the morning but Gordon was the other way around. He milked after tea so his cows had the longer stretch by day. When our milking machine was put in the men stayed overnight as it couldn't be done in a day, and Gordon was sitting with his dying father. That was in 1952. Yours was put in first, wasn't it?'

'Yes, and we had electricity before you. Before that I used a petrol engine.'

'We didn't have electricity until 1960 when I got married, so I know what it's like to live with oil lamps. We had the bathroom and toilet two years later. The 'little house' in the garden is now a listed loo!'

John said, 'You had your Dutch barn before us, didn't you?'

'Ours was 1966.'

---

[56] John's last collection of milk was 30 Sept and Gordon's 8 Nov 1976

'Mine was a few years later. Before that everything was in ricks. Marjorie could stack away 1000 bales a day, that's 25 tons.'

'I can remember Gordon and Arthur going down to thatch your ricks.'

'That would be the straw one after thrashing. I kept one of sheaves for feeding and there would be about three of hay covered with plastic. We had about 1000 bales of hay in a rick.'

John continued, 'When I first started we had 1½ days thrashing. We had a big roast on the first day and pasties on the second day. It needed 18 men for a thrashing and we all went round helping each other. We couldn't seat that number round the kitchen table so I took a door off the cows-house and we covered that with a white cloth in the front room. Then I got a combine, the first in this area, and did everything myself.'

'When did you buy your first tractor?' I asked.

'Just before we went up to Trevail. It was second hand, a Fordson. They had no hydraulics or power steering to start with. Then I had an International, then a Nuffield and I had two Leylands when I finished.'

'Gordon's first one was an Allis Chalmers. They ran on TVO in those days (tractor vaporising oil), now we use diesel. It had a hand throttle and was dead easy for me to drive but he had to start it with a cranking handle. One day he went to the doctor because his hand hurt and he said the tractor had kicked him. Dr. Slack said, 'why didn't you kick it back?' Another time Gordon told the doctor he fell when climbing back over the hedge after shutting the gate. It was a locum who said, 'Why didn't you go the other side before closing the gate?' Gordon was not very good at explaining things but the gate could only be shut from one side. It was propped across the gap-way leaning on the hedges and then rocks built up to hold it in place.'

'A milking herd needs the same number of followers,' said John. 'I kept my heifer calves for that and sold the steers at 15 months for finishing. I had 30 breeding sows as well. Penzance market was the place for dairy cattle but it was Camborne for beef. Helston took everything but had a big pig market. Truro was best for sheep.'

'Well, I didn't know that,' I said.

'Farming was quite good then, not like all the regulations and paper work you have now.'

'When did we join the European Union?' I asked, at the mention of paper work.

'Wasn't it about 1973?' he replied. 'I'm glad I retired in 1982.'

1980-2000 Jean (me) and Rose

In 1980 Gordon became an Old Age Pensioner with a dependent wife and four dependent children. The children all got full grants for their further education. Rose came back from agricultural college in 1987 and the next year she organised the change from making small baled hay to big baled silage. She says that was one of the biggest changes on the farm. Hay has to dry for a week or more and too much rain in that time can ruin it. Silage can be done in a few days and a bit of damp doesn't matter. Rose kept a few sheep and reared orphan lambs for farmers who did not want them. We'd wake up in the morning to find one or more soggy orphans outside the door more dead than alive. She'd bring them in, wrap them up and put them in the bottom oven of the Rayburn. When they revived she gave them a bottle of milk and soon they were strong enough to go outside. She had 10 each in three pens in the old cows-house with milk in self-feeders. In 1987 the farm was designated an Environmentally Sensitive Area and things gradually improved financially. The first year we were paid £4000 for maintaining our hedges and not clearing any of the boulders from our small fields. Now there are several books of instructions on how to maintain the landscape.

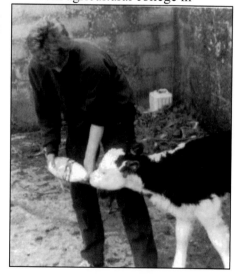

Figure 6 Rose feeding a calf

Gordon died in 1993, with his boots on, aged 77. It was a great shock to all of us but I just stuck my head down and stuck in. Over the next two years people in the trade learnt to respect me and the price of my calves increased. When passports came in I thought it was so ridiculous I photographed all our cows. It has proved useful though. If we think a cow is missing we get out her photo to check what we are looking for. I spent days looking for Indi once, till I checked her photo and found she was a white cow, not a black one. Our cows are all named, another of Rose's ideas. She began with A and names must be short enough to go on an ear tag. This year we have reached N and the black one is Noir.

Left: Figure 7 An orphan lamb in bottom oven watched by Mint Sauce, the cat. Right: Figure 8 Lambs with self-feeder which is a bucket of milk surrounded by teats

The cattle are checked every day, two or three times a day when the cows are calving. I make lists of everything. We can take them out into the fields and tick off all the cows, or all the calves. With a hundred of each it's rather too much to do in one day. Calves are tagged in both ears the day they are born. Sometimes we have 2 or 3 calves in the morning and 2 or 3 in the afternoon. That lasts for about three months, February, March and April. I always have two hired bulls booked for Towednack Feast (April 28th) and so the year goes round again.

Figure 9 Rose repairing a hedge in 1999

I think Rose is marvellous. She's great at welding and does most of the servicing on our farm machinery. When the National Trust did some fencing she went down to help. She's always rebuilding our granite hedges and her biggest project was 40 metres out the Big Eagle's Nest Field. She spent all one summer bedding in foundations, lifting great rocks with the tractor and infilling with smaller stones and earth. It could be seen from the road and those who know what a skilled job it is, stopped to admire her work. Some farmers have the vet to castrate their calves and de-horn them, but Rose does all that. De-horning is done at six weeks.

The cattle TB test (for tuberculosis) is the biggest event every year for us now. Each year I bring all my cows into the yard and they are secured in the cattle crush one at a time. The vet injects them twice as I record their ear numbers, the skin thickness and other details. Every other year blood samples are taken and I label the bottles for the vet. These are tested for brucellosis. When we were milking it was easier as the cows were used to being tied up. Now they

41

Figure 10 TB testing in 1987.

don't like coming in and their calves jump everywhere. Neighbours come to help for the day and the weather is usually wet and windy! On the second day, when the skin readings are taken again, the cattle are even less keen to go through the crush.

The year after Gordon died one of my cows reacted to the TB test and I wondered if the farm would pull through the disaster. The cow was slaughtered and a movement restriction put on my herd. Sixty days later the whole herd was tested again, and so on until we had two clear tests. It was 24 years since we last had a reactor but then the milk cheque came in every month. This time, with a beef herd, I was not allowed to sell anything.

For beef farmers who sell calves every year it would be a great strain having two crops of calves on the farm. The cows need extra attention, the herd needs extra fodder, there are problems of income and anxiety. Luckily we survived but every year I don't sleep properly for the week of the TB test.

We'd nearly stamped out TB in the 1980s. When badgers became protected they spread up-country and so did the TB. In 2000 MAFF (Ministry of Agriculture, Fisheries and Food) tried to catch all the badgers in our area but they only caught 20 per cent and then they didn't test them. Our badgers were left alone.

We plan our TB test for before Christmas when all the calves have been sold and before the cows are too heavy in calf. Figure 10 shows the cattle crush attached to the tractor to keep it steady. Ann-Marie (my eldest) has pulled a bar against the cow's neck to keep her still. All cooking is done in advance. I make an enormous stew, fruit crumble, trifles,

Figure 11 Croust at Wicca, 1989.

heavy cake and sponges. Sometimes I buy pasties for the second day. We're up early on the day and the cows are fed silage in the nearest field. After an hour they've eaten most of it and we bring the cows into the yard. Rose and Sam tie gates on top of the gates in case a cow makes a bid for freedom.

Figure 12 Grandson Michael, aged five, helps with the feeding at Wicca, December 1999

At 9.30 we're ready to start, the vet arrives and so do the helpers. Halfway through we stop for croust (elevenses) and have lunch when we've finished. The vet usually leaves at 2. One year Kate, the vet, was so cold we put her in the oven, or rather, we sat her beside the Rayburn with her feet in the bottom oven. We spend the afternoon clearing up.

On the second day, if we're lucky, we can go straight through. In the middle of the morning we stop for croust of saffron cake etc. Figure 11 shows Tom (my youngest), John Hardern the vet, Gordon and Rose (from left to right). The hens will eat anything so the lid is on the biscuit tin. I try to give everyone a present of either our beef or a home baked cake. If the TB test is clear we can breathe again until the next one. Now that Rose has two small children we have to juggle them with all the work on the farm. Figure 12 shows another grandson, five year old Michael, helping with the feeding.

The paper-work today is unending and would be better called 'Farming Frustrations'. In my diary for January 2000[57] I wrote that it had doubled and doubled again in the last few years. It takes 5 minutes to load a cull cow on the lorry but two days to do the paperwork. Without the right papers an animal is worthless!

That month I updated my records for the Suckler Cow Premium (89.1 cows, later reduced to 86.6 when MAFF creamed off 3 per cent for some reason), and the Hill Livestock Compensatory Allowance (even fewer cows). The southern part of my farm is in a Less Favoured Area where I am allowed to keep 82.49 cows. As the boundary follows the footpath which goes through the middle of my fields, I stand on the path and every time more than 82.49 cows cross it, I wave them back.

When the calves are born I have to apply for their passports which are like a book. The rules for them can change several times a year. They must be born with two ears and have a tag in each ear or they are illegal and cannot be traded! Other correspondence that January informed me that I had a new herd number and from June 30th all calves would need 14 digit ear numbers: and, surprise, MAFF had changed their 'phone numbers AGAIN. For every animal on my farm I must record the ear number, birth, sex, breed, dam, sire, retag number, if any, and subsidies claimed. Then enter the total number of animals in nine different columns for every day of the year. Next year all my calves will be born on Sunday and then the age totals will only change once a week instead of every day!

One winter afternoon two men came to inspect some of our ESA hedges. We kept them talking until nearly dark and then pointed them in the direction of the cliff! If MAFF makes a mistake we are penalised which is why I spend so much time checking their print-outs. In December 1999 I received an updated map of my farm which took four days to check. I carefully listed all the mistakes and sent it back. For over six years I was correcting their mistakes before the last 0.02 of a hectare was agreed. The worst forms of all are the IACS (Integrated Administration Control System for the fields) which come in March and take two months to sort out! The latest bit of nonsense is that every time the word 'farmer' is used they follow it with 'shall mean a natural or legal person'. I say I am a farmeress so I'm unnatural and illegal!

Arthur Mann's Talk

Figure 13 Thrashing at Trewey, September 9th 1996.
Left to right; Arthur, Nora with their son Harry, Harry's children Jenny and David and Harry's wife Caroline

---

[57] CRO ref. WIZEN

Arthur Mann was born in 1927 and his family came to Trewey in 1945, the same Michaelmas that John Loosemore started at Higher Trevail. Figure 13 shows Arthur with his wife Nora, their son Harry, Harry's children Jenny and David, and Harry's wife Caroline (left to right). In 2002 Arthur gave an excellent description of field work[58].

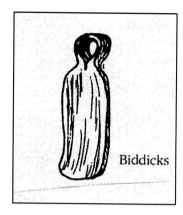

Biddicks

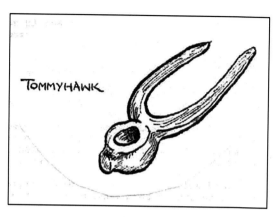

TOMMYHAWK

This is a piggle for digging out ditches and also for digging up the big horse thistles (see illustration of biddicks). When I was a teenager we used to clear the ditches and pull it away by horse and cart into a corner of the field. We left them to rot down, which takes 6 to 9 months. Then we used to put cart-loads of farm manure on the pile. We used to mix it with a shovel and tommy hawk (see illustration) to loosen it up so it would mix better. We used to call that short dung or some of the older people would call it short dressing. After a couple of months it had to be loaded by hand onto a cart and pulled out into the field in small piles about 6 paces apart again to be spread by the heaval (eval) by hand. Sometimes we would plant flat pole cabbage in the pile if it was taking longer to rot. They would keep it clean.

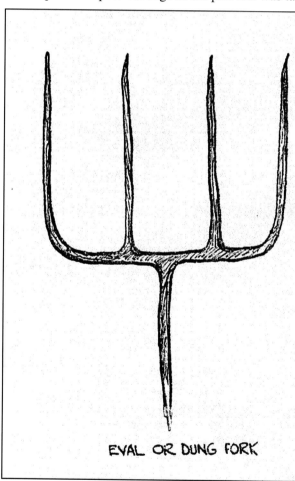

EVAL OR DUNG FORK

We used horses for ploughing and tilling the fields until 1960. We had our first tractor in 1939 but used that for other work, like disc harrowing and pulling the wagons. They didn't plough so deep then as they do now. This is why the fields didn't get so weedy in those days; not like now when you get more weeds because of tractors ploughing so deep.

All the artificial manure used was sown by hand. There were no fertilizer spreaders when we came to Trewey. We had a pan with 2 handles with a piece of rope fastened to each one and then looped around your neck. And we sewed the seed the same way. You had to walk in a straight line at the same pace and throw out the seed, first to one side and then the other, with exactly the same swing. If you went faster or slower, or threw the seed further it would come up in stripes and all your neighbours would see it. The seed mustn't be thicker or thinner in any one place.

In the spring time you did a lot of it for days on end. Our neck and shoulders used to get rather sore. We used to sow the corn all by hand for years, until the drills became popular. We tilled mainly oats in those days. I've heard my father say before the binder came, they used to cut most of it with a scythe. Then it was the

---

[58] Arthur and Nora Mann gave a talk to the Cornwall Association of Local Historians in February 2002 and their notes were reproduced in the next CALH Journal.

women's job to take up the corn into sheaves for the men to bind using some of the corn. They then would build them into knee mows (small ricks). When the binder became popular it was wonderful to have it cut and put into sheaves and tied all in one movement.

After the corn was pulled away from the corn arrish [stubble] we used to scuffle the fields with horses. An ordinary scuffler had 9 feet on it. Quite easy to pull. This is when we used to break in young horses. Starting them to work, on the lighter jobs. We used to trim all our hedges, with a hook and cuff made from an old rubber boot.

BUSSA.

Faggots of furze (gorse) were cut to go under the ricks of hay and corn. After the rick was used, the faggots were put in some place to keep dry for burning in the open chimneys. Also we cut ferns [bracken] for bedding the cattle. We called it, if the weather was nice, a fernie scat [cut].

We used to cut the hay with a machine called a reaper, pulled by 2 horses. It was hard work for the horses. If it was very sunny the flies would bite awful. Sometimes we would wipe the horses with a cloth soaked in paraffin, which would help a lot. After the hay was cut for 2 or 3 days depending on the weather, we would turn it over by hand with pikes. After another day or two, we would take out another machine called a kicker. Also pulled by a horse, that kicker would toss the hay up to let the breeze get to it. If the weather was kind to us we could start pulling it into a rick with a horse and wagon after about a week or 9 days.

It's much easier now with modern equipment to cut with big tractor mowers. Also we now have different things to move the hay around. We can bale it into big round bales. Silage is the most common crop now. A lot of people get 3 crops a year. Some very modern equipment is being used now. I'm afraid I don't have much to do with it. It's like hay, the better the weather, the better the crop.

The horses I've got have been bred up from the horses that my dad had before the First World War. He used to take his horse to camp. He was a volunteer in the Devon and Somerset Yeomanry. I don't think many people can say they've got the same line of breeding horses so long ago as that.

Nora Mann's Talk

Nora had known Arthur all her life and they were married in 1950. Arthur had lived at Merthyr Farm, Morvah, four miles further west. Nora's family farmed at Keigwin, next door but one. Nora's talk in 2002 was about milk and butter making in the 1930s.

I would like to tell you about a few memories of my childhood days. There were no milking machines in those days. You sat on a three-legged stool on the right hand side of the cow with a milking pail held between your knees, hoping the cow would stay quiet long enough for you to accomplish the job of getting all the milk safely in the pail or bucket. We used to wear a towser (apron made of an old sack). When all the milk was gathered from the cows it was carried to the dairy. It was

Scotch hands

strained through a muslin gauze and put in a separator where the cream came out of one spout and the skimmed milk came out of the other.

When eventually a full pail of cream was collected it was transferred into the butter churn. It was sealed down by a big cover with four clamps screwed down tight. In the cover was a

Butter tub

small round glass window. This little window was to let you know when the cream was turning into butter. To start with, the little window was clouded over with the cream but when the cream turned into butter the little window became clear.

The churn was turned around by hand using a handle. This process would take anything from half to one hour according to the temperature and the weather. This could become a very tedious job when the weather was too warm.

When the butter was made it was then washed several times before being salted. To get all the buttermilk out after each washing, you pulled out a wood plug at the bottom of the churn and caught the buttermilk in a huge pail. This was then fed to the pigs.

On rare occasions when the butter was too soft, I have seen my mother and father place the butter into a large butter tub and lower it down 30 feet into a peath, which is a deep well, and let it rest just on top of the water to harden the butter up before they could begin to weigh it up into 1 pound or ½ pound pats using the scotch hands (see illustration).

Thursday was market day in Penzance so the butter was taken in a butter basket, also eggs in a basket. We went by horse and trap. This was the main source of income but was supplemented by the sale of poultry and home produced pork. When there was too much butter to be taken to market, the surplus was put into stone glazed jars (bussas) with some extra salt added and eaten by the family in winter months.

Butter churn

Looking back over the years I'd say my parents were very pleased when the Milk Marketing Board was formed in 1933 and the milk was collected from the farm in milk churns. How things have changed since then. Milking machines are now in use, the milk goes from the cow into stainless steel pipes being strained and cooled on the way before reaching the large ice-cold milk tank. The milk has to be cooled to a certain temperature before the milk tanker will take it. Surely this has to be much easier than milking by hand and having to make cream and butter to sell as in the earlier days.

Figure 14 Cows during the eclipse, August 1999. As the sky darkened the cows gently mooed, calling their calves towards them as they would at dusk. After a couple of minutes, as the light came back, they continued to graze as normal.

Postscript (Jean): No one has mentioned cream which farmers make for themselves from the rich Guernsey milk. Everyone else left the milk for the cream to rise first but I never bothered. I had about six pints of milk in a shallow enamel bowl and just put it straight on the Rayburn. It stayed at the cool end all evening. The milk must be hot enough to cook the cream but not hot enough to boil. I carefully carried the bowl down the dairy for the night and next morning skimmed off the cream. The milk left was richer than any milk you get in a silver top bottle today. Some called it scalded cream or clotted cream but we just called it cream because we didn't know any other. Of course, we had cream with everything, and any left-over went in the mashed potato.

Not many make cream for sale these days because of all the regulations but before 1933 clotted cream was sold to local dairies. My husband Gordon would have a pan of cream balanced on the petrol tank of his motorbike and ride down St Ives with it. He would stop outside the shop and wait for someone to come out and take the balanced bowl from his bike. No rules on health and safety then!

6. *Corpus-Christi Fair*

Ann Altree

Corpus-Christi Fair was granted by the charter of 1614.[59] The Fair, held in Penzance, always opens on the Thursday after Trinity Sunday and therefore depends on the date of Easter each year.

My grandfather, WH Eva, remembered that in 1881, when 10 years old, the great treat of the year was Corpus-Christi Fair. He used to go with friends out to Eastern Green to watch the arrival of the wagons and all tried to guess what would be at the Fair that year. Around this time small sideshows included a Fat Woman and the Wild Man of Borneo who was kept in a cage, for the public's entertainment. There were also steam roundabouts. The *Cornishman* of 9 June 1898 mentions that the Whitsun Fair at Redruth had a new innovation in the shape of a cinematograph, which was well supported. It is almost certain that they travelled on to Penzance for the Corpus-Christi Fair and attracted equally large audiences. The film by this time was very 'rain-stormed' with its constant use and also flickered a great deal, which was very tiring on the eyes[60].

Captain Rowland's Moving Pictures and Lions (Courtesy Morrab Library)

In 1899 Professor Anderton of Anderton and Rowland acquired a projector and started to entertain the public. This new innovation was sweeping the country. He combined a programme of moving pictures and performing lions.[61]

Corpus-Christi Fair first boasted a Biograph entertainment in 1900.[62] In this year on opening day there was a lot of rain and slushy mud but this did not put anyone off going to the Recreation Ground and on that Thursday there was a large number of people attending. Some of the sideshows, small theatres and circuses were missing compared with previous years, but there were many shooting galleries and coconut shies. Messrs Hancock had their lovely set of roundabout horses and a switchback, which were enjoyed by all. A Mr. Brewer also had a set of horses to ride on. The Fair this

---

[59] Pool: 32, 220.
[60] Eva: Box 1, Item 8.
[61] De Vey. For full bibliographical details, see the Bibliography on pp. 113-116.
[62] *Cornishman* 21 June 1900: 3, col 4.

year had three organs situated very close together but as reported, they produced a very weird and wonderful result. For anyone feeling hungry, the Hot Chip potatoes were very popular, and Mr George Hamlyn of Penzance sold pure sweets and savoury gingerbreads

Playing the Melodies Grand Organ (Courtesy Ann Altree)

Some of the old fairground entertainments were changing; innovations were taking place like the Bioscope. It was so exciting—to see people and moving images on a screen! It was one of the biggest crazes in the early 1900s. Anderton and Rowland commissioned a new show in 1906 and then concentrated on moving pictures without the lions. This they called Anderton and Rowlands Grand Empire Palace. To generate the power needed, steam engines were used. At night hundreds of miniature light bulbs lit the front; as the music played the colour of the bulbs changed. The 2½-hour programme of films and entertainment cost 4d, 6d or 1/-. The Grand Empire Palace travelled the West Country until 1914, two years after the Savoy Cinema started in Penzance (see appendix at the end of this chapter).

My grandfather, WH Eva, attended Corpus Christi Fair for 75 years until he was 85 years old. When my mother and aunt were children he used to take them on the Saturday afternoon but always went back in the evening to see the Fair lit up. The rides did not appeal to him as much as all the stalls and sideshows—this is where he spent most of his time.

In the early 1950s I used to go to Corpus-Christi Fair with my mother, father and of course Grandpa, who was then 80 years old. As we walked from the end of Tolver Road, each side was packed with stalls, fortune tellers and cheapjacks selling their wares. Some people used to get food bargains from them, but others did not do so well. At night the road was lit by the many lights on the stalls. When you entered the gates of the Recreation Ground, it was full of people, stalls, rides and sideshows. Situated around the perimeter were the showmen's caravans; they were very elaborate. I was lucky to go inside one of these in Redruth; it was beautiful.

Helter Skelter at the Royal Cornwall Show
(Courtesy Raymond Altree)

In front of the caravans were the sideshows. Like my grandfather I was not keen on the rides but loved the stalls and sideshows. I remember going into the Hall of Mirrors; in some you looked very short and fat while the next mirror you looked into you might be very tall and then everyone had a good laugh as you looked at yourself and other people. After this we would go and see the Snake Lady, who sat in the centre of the tent in a large glass box with the snakes—which were slithering all over her body.

The Fair always had boxing booths at this time; we never went into these, probably my mother, father and grandfather thought it was not suitable for me. The dancing girls were outside the theatre shows to draw in an audience. Once inside you had to wait a long time before the show started as a full house was always wanted before the start.

The rides at this time always included at least two sets of dodgems. The theory was to dodge the other cars but this never happened as everyone always wanted to bump into someone they knew. The Helter Skelter was always fun. Everyone was given a mat when they paid their money, went inside and started the climb to the top. When you arrived there, you put your mat down and sat on it before you were left at the top without a mat! Then you made your way round and round to the bottom and always wanted another go. What a good view you had from the top.

On the Big Wheel you usually sat two per seat. The fairground attendants would often swing the seats to make them rock. It was not anything like the London Eye which is 450 feet high but at this time it was the highest fair ride—you saw things you did not think possible.

Around this time the Waltzers were fairly new; the turning of the bucket seats and the motion of going around and up and down made most people feel quite sick. Then there was the Noah's Ark where you sat on wooden wild animals and as well as going around, you were riding up and down: always a very fast ride. But the last ride on a Saturday evening was always at full speed and everyone on it had a hard job to stay on. The time for this would depend on how many people were still at the Fair, but it could be anywhere between 11 p.m. and midnight.

Waltzers at the Wharf side (Courtesy Ann Altree)

Between 1960 and 1980 the Fairs did not alter very much although there were a few more new attractions. I remember one particular stall where you could win a goldfish; around the centre were small, clear bags hanging up with goldfish inside. Around these was moving water in which were yellow ducks with numbers on the bottom and a metal loop on their backs. You paid your money and were given a crook on a pole and then you tried to hook a duck; depending on the number written on the bottom you managed to win a fish or not. In one particular year, I managed to win three so I had to buy a proper bowl with weed to keep them in; you could get these at the Fair. I had those goldfish for a long time.

In the late 60s and 70s I went to see the Wall of Death. Inside the tent were raised wooden benches situated around a large globe, a very strong mesh-like construction. These shows started at certain times of the day and were usually packed with people. When the show started the performer rode into the tent, through an opening into the globe on a motor bike and the opening then closed. He then would ride around the globe walls and then almost vertically over the top. Then a motor bike with side-car was introduced. Usually this was done with two people, one in the side-car, the other on the motor bike. At the end of the show a member of the audience would be invited to ride in the side-car. Sometimes one person would be brave enough to do this. I would go and see this at least twice; it was the excitement that delighted everyone. The Wall of Death was introduced into the fairs in the 1930s. In 2002 there were only 3 of these left in Great Britain. No longer do our fairs travel around with the Wall of Death.[63]

Bingo stalls made an appearance, the craze of the time. There were two if not three at Corpus-Christi. Everyone sat around the stall and had to wait until every seat was taken. If you were lucky enough to win, any prize on the stall was yours; the other people left with nothing. All through the years the fairs had stalls selling toffee apples, sweets, toffee and candy floss. Beef burgers and fish and chips in later years were usually situated just in front of the gates or just inside the Recreation Ground.

---

[63] Calladine

Toys and Gallopers for children (Courtesy Ann Altree)

In 1999, after quite a number of years not attending Corpus-Christi Fair, what a shock I had! The Fair had gone from being a huge affair to one that was less than half of what it was. Gone were the cheapjacks and stalls lining the end of Tolver Road and outside the Recreation Ground. Inside, as you walked around, the Dodgems and Waltzers were still there but the other rides were designed for another generation. Most of the stalls had disappeared and new ones had taken their place. The Fair moved from the Recreation Ground where it had been for many years to the Wharf car park in 2005. The rides consisted of the Twister, the Big Wheel, still doing the rounds at fairs, one Terminator, two sets of Dodgems, the Waltzers which have been so popular for so many years, and children's rides. The stalls included darts, and slot machines were very evident. There was also a Crazy Castle and Fun House. In this year, the Gladiator steam engine and organ were present, creating a lot of interest.

The Terminator in Penzance (Courtesy Ann Altree)

Everyone still enjoys the Fair when it comes to Penzance, but not as my grandfather would remember it. I can hear him say: 'It's not what it used to be'. But probably the children of today would not agree and we hope Corpus-Christi Fair will go on for many years.

Left: The Gladiator steam engine which was built in 1909. She was at the Smithfield show that year, having been delivered to Anderton and Rowland in Wales where she was to be used in conjunction with their Bioscope film show. The Gladiator still travels to fairs and the picture was taken by Ann Altree at Penzance in 2005.

Appendix: More about the cinema in Penzance

The Savoy opened on Friday 29 November 1912.[64] It is the oldest continuously running cinema in Great Britain and it has never closed over the now 95 years. It even stayed open during the two world wars. It was opened by the Mayor of Penzance Mr. A. K. Barnett and was a most beautiful cinema. On either side of the stage were lovely ferns. The colours of the interior were panels of silk paper in green, cream and gold. There were red plush tip-up seats for 400 people, and carpets. The ventilation by electric fans was situated under the roof to get rid of the smoke. Below the stage was an area for an orchestra to play. The film projectors were the very latest machines. The building itself, before becoming a cinema, was called the Victoria Hall.

Competition came in 1915 when another hall in Parade Street converted into a cinema called the Picturedrome (later called the Regal). In February 1958 this building made way for the Inland Revenue Offices. The Ritz in Queen Street, of Art Deco design, opened as a cinema in 1936 and could seat up to one thousand people. In 1966 the Ritz closed as a cinema to become a Bingo Hall which is still there today.

The Savoy in 2007 is still a cinema but now multi-screen with the addition of a bar and restaurant. But without the Fairs, would we have had these three cinemas in Penzance? It was because of the Biograph and moving pictures being shown earlier at the Fairs that the craze took off.

---

[64] Calladine.

7. Groping in the Dark?

Dawn Walker

West Cornwall is an internationally important archaeological landscape. Its sites and monuments range from remains of the mining industry (recently recognised as a World Heritage site), back in time to the standing stones, circles and burial chambers built in the middle and late Neolithic, and earlier. The major ancient monuments had been well known, both in Cornwall and the wider world, since the earliest travellers and topographers such as Leland, Camden and Carew.[65] In the seventeenth century, John Norden, the great mapmaker, added many details about the megalithic monuments. However, as with his contemporaries, his main objective was to map the estates and mansions of his socially aspiring sponsors and any ancient monuments were something of an afterthought and often purely decorative. It was William Borlase, the rector of Ludgvan writing in the 1750s, who made the first serious academic study of the archaeology of West Cornwall, and in particular of West Penwith. He was scrupulous in his measured plans and notes of the monuments he studied, so much so that even twentieth-century archaeologists refer to them and quote them in their professional reports, and his system of cataloguing by parish is still in use. When it came to trying to interpret the monuments, however, he believed that the interested collectors of ancient objects and commentators on the great stone monuments were merely groping in the dark when they attempted to date or explain the nature of their finds and sites. He was of course writing before Darwin and as a churchman must have accepted that the earth was not more than ten thousand years old. Fortunately, his wide general and scientific knowledge, together with his huge correspondence with others like him, did mean that although the monuments remained basically mysterious, he knew they were not unique: he was able, for example, to compare them with similar monuments in Pembrokeshire[66]. His recognition of this similarity led in time to the linking of Cornish quoits or cromlechs with those in France,[67] so that by the twentieth century it was clear that they were just part of a much wider distribution along the coastlines of Western Europe.

Chun Quoit (Courtesy HES)

---

[65] Leland; Camden; Carew. For full bibliographical details, see the Bibliography on pp. 113-116.
[66] Borlase: 409.
[67] Lewis: 409-412.

53

Nineteenth-century Cornwall reflected the social and economic changes in the rest of the country—a great increase in population, wealth, travel and education, especially amongst the burgeoning middle class—and the increasing pace of discovery and interest in 'antiquities' became notable. Changes in farm machinery meant that small artefacts were appearing in fields being ploughed more deeply; people exploring both coast and countryside were now much more aware of ancient items and were on the lookout for them. Collecting flint and stone tools (often described as 'weapons') was a popular hobby and, where coins or metal objects were concerned, working-men also were now aware of their potential value and added to the watchful eyes, whilst the building of roads and railways increased their opportunities. The finding of the gold cup at Rillaton (near Minions) in 1837 certainly added to the general enthusiasm. As education and literacy improved in West Cornwall, the publication of descriptions of ancient sites and finds increased. Richard Thomas, an engineer and surveyor from Falmouth, wrote over fifty articles for the *West Briton* between 1850 and 1852, adding to the growing interest.

Amongst the educated classes in West Cornwall in this century, it was thought to be a good thing to become a member of at least one learned society. Members attended lectures on a wide range of subjects including what was becoming 'archaeology' rather than 'antiquities'. At the end of the Napoleonic Wars, the Cornwall Literary and Philosophical Institution was founded (from 1821 known as the Royal Institution of Cornwall): fortunately for subsequent researchers it published annual journals. Geology and natural history were popular topics, but between 1900 and 1977 local archaeology featured in thirty of the issues. The comments of the authors—mostly amateurs in the early issues—reveal clearly the views current at the time. For example in the Annual Report of 1909,[68] a midden was reported found on Godrevy Down and Mr Rogers argued that flint chips were as good evidence of the presence of ancient man as perfectly finished weapons were—'despite disagreements in earlier journals'. Two interesting views are shown here: firstly, that flint finds were usually described as weapons rather than the now recognised mixture of flint tools for everyday purposes, with a small percentage just as likely to be used for hunting as for fighting; and secondly, that the process of working flint was not fully understood, if some members still believed that flint flakes were not a positive indication of human work.

The journals of the early 1900s also show that RIC members were reading widely. One member, reviewing a book on the Stone Ages, disagreed with the author's argument that there was no satisfactory evidence that man lived before the glacial period and was able to quote considerable alternative theories and evidence. The RIC had a strong influence on the growing appreciation of archaeology in West Cornwall, with its programme of lectures and demonstrations and, as with similar groups elsewhere in the country, worked towards founding a library and a museum and offered free or cheap educational classes to working people. Thurston Peter, President in 1914, was determined that after the war militarism would be abolished and culture re-asserted, and that it was the RIC's duty to be involved in this. The Institution's museum opened on its present site in Truro in 1919 and still flourishes as the Royal Cornwall Museum.

Members of the various societies had organised numerous daytrips, some long and arduous, but the twentieth century saw the development of the omnibus, the arrival of charabancs and, by the first World War, private cars, which made life easier for those wanting to visit ancient monuments. It also saw the wider use of the camera: both local people and tourists began to take souvenir photographs posed in front of famous monuments which were clearly now of general public interest. Some visitors came to West Cornwall in order to see ancient monuments and kept diaries and photograph albums: there is one such in the Penlee Museum, made by two ladies in August 1928. Tourist guides and travel books for the area proliferated. Writing in 1912, Stone[69] emphasised the extreme antiquity of West Cornwall. He described ancient stone monuments as rude and rudimentary yet clearly bearing evidence that they were very ancient artefacts; however he thought some of the monoliths were relatively modern, put up for cattle to scratch themselves on. At the time he was writing, theories of the original builders of the stone circles, tombs and monoliths and their possible purposes were still heavily affected by the religious and classical viewpoints which were such an important aspect of the education system of the upper and middle classes in the early 1900s. Oxford and Cambridge, and their

---

[68] Rogers: 238
[69] Stone

feeder public and grammar schools, continued to give a classical education that in many respects was unchanged from that given in the later stages of the Roman Empire;[70] both the Enlightenment and the French Revolution had passed them by and everything taught was dominated by the dead hand of Anglican Christianity. The distant past had to fit into contemporary theology—although the earth's 10,000-year age-limit could no longer be supported. The Stone, Bronze and Iron Ages had been devised to general agreement, since it seemed a logical progression of human achievement to move from the use of natural local materials to those requiring increasingly complex procuring and processing, but reference to biblical and classical studies was still common; the ancient remains in West Cornwall were commonly associated with the Druids and Celts of Julius Caesar's description.

However, in 1897 archaeology had first appeared within the study of Classics in Cambridge, although inspired by sculpture brought back from Grand Tours rather than by home-grown items; there were also many serious collectors of coins, especially Roman, and Egyptian archaeology was of course widely reported and admired. The megaliths of West Cornwall did indeed appear rudimentary in comparison and unattractive to anyone considering a career in archaeology. Local enthusiasts were not however deterred and it is quite surprising that despite the wholesale collecting throughout the nineteenth century it could still be reported to the RIC in 1919 that prehistoric flints and other stone implements were plentifully distributed over the fields, particularly around St Levan, St Buryan and Sennen.[71] One notable collector, J.G. Marsden, had collected several thousand and had recognised that flints previously described as 'cones' were in fact cores, from which blades had been struck. He also commented on the use of beach pebbles as raw materials and thought that flints could be dated by the depth of their patination. Many finds were recorded in diaries and published, and some found their way to museums, but this general collecting was still a long way from the field-walking techniques of the later twentieth century where careful, detailed mapping of surface finds are vital indicators to archaeologists.

By the 1920s, methods were improving rapidly. Flints found at Camborne Beacon were carefully described in their context (i.e. depth below surface, type of soils, etc) and the finder was not confused by a nearby deposit of gun flints.[72] Members frequently reported their own private excavations or 'diggings', which were a definite improvement on the popular Sunday-afternoon entertainment of the eighteenth- and nineteenth-century digs, where a vertical hole would be dug into the nearest barrow in the hope of finding treasure, and then roughly filled in again, with pottery

Alsia Well - with ribbons, coins and bangle (Courtesy Glyn Richards)

fragments discarded as rubbish. Marsden and some friends dug into a round barrow at St Buryan[73] noting that it had already been opened. They made measurements and recorded finds carefully. Notably at one stage, the excavator was removing layers of soil one at a time and making observations, in this way identifying a floor with pits and being able to locate finds to a specific level. All excavation is destructive, but these early twentieth-century investigations did at least leave some records and in most cases sites were carefully restored. Much more alarming was the very longstanding damage being done to monuments and sites either by neglect or actual destruction. The standing stones of circles were a particular temptation for farmers looking for new gateposts or for lintels over doors and windows. Even in the 1850s, Richard Thomas had reported the continual loss of

[70] Stray: 123-34
[71] Marsden (1919): 483.
[72] Marsden (1921): 48-55.
[73] Marsden (1922): 169-174.

barrows, and farmers continued to wish to destroy them: they interfered with modern ploughing and the heaped-up soil was also potentially useful to spread over fields and add to their fertility. It was unfortunate that explosives were readily available in the mining districts and were just the thing for breaking up intractable monoliths.

To some extent, ancient monuments were protected by superstition. Many were accounted for in local myths as being 'magic' in origin and it was believed that it was unlucky to move or damage them, especially those which might offer a benefit such as a cure for sick children or, in the case of some Holy Wells, a cure for bad eyes. Hencken[74] wrote the first twentieth-century synthesis of current knowledge of Cornish archaeology and reported the widespread belief that certain old stones could move, drink and speak at given times. Stone had been told the story of a farmer who sold some old stones from his land for the building of Penzance harbour, and who never thereafter prospered. This mystical view of ancient monuments is known even today (2007). Alsia Well (see photograph on previous page) is one of several in West Penwith that can be found with offerings of coins and pieces of cloth tied onto nearby branches. In the 1990s a busload of ladies returning from Penzance shopping were entertained by the sight of a nude man dancing around the Merry Maidens, no doubt for some serious ritualistic purpose.

Wartime evacuees visiting Chysuaster (Courtesy Morrab Library)

Fortunately, from the late 1920s, an increasing number of local people and visiting archaeologists were taking a more scientific interest in the finds and ancient monuments. In the 1930s, local excavation reports were being published in a national journal (*Archaeology*) and in 1935 the West Cornwall Field Club was formed (later to become the Cornwall Archaeological Society):[75] a retired army officer, Fred Hirst, had involved the Cornwall Excavations Committee with the Ministry of Works dig at Chysauster. This and subsequent excavations aroused huge public interest in West Cornwall. The Wayside Museum at Zennor was started by Hirst and the later creation of the Cornish Archaeological Society had no problem in finding members.

---

[74] Hencken
[75] CAS.

The debate over the purpose of fogous was well under way (and still not settled in 2007) and numerous excavations such as that at Chun Castle (see photograph below) and Chysauster[76] were offering new evidence and ideas on the origins of hill forts and settlements. Scientific methods of excavation, originating from Egyptian archaeology in the nineteenth century, were now accepted as the desirable standard, and the days of digging random holes in barrows were thankfully over. Approximate dates could now be ascribed to more detailed archaeological ages, although there was not yet a clear view of the Mesolithic (described by Hencken as 'the dreary epipalealithic cultures'). Prehistoric Cornwall's trade links with overseas, particularly the Mediterranean, were at last recognised when the thirties saw the first modern excavations at Tintagel and Magor.

World War II slowed the development of archaeology in West Cornwall, but this was more than made up by the major national developments in the next fifty to sixty years, which naturally affected our county. Immediately after the war, the political and economic situation of Britain made large-scale overseas excavations difficult, but there were some favourable factors at home. Bomb-damage in some cities had opened sites where excavation had never before been practicable. The arrival of television and the growth of the media in general encouraged public interest; for example, I was working in the City in 1954 and remember the excitement of the discovery of the Temple of Mithras which was headline news. It was possibly one of the first times in this country when archaeologists had to deal with large numbers of people wanting to peer over their shoulders and see things being dug up. A popular radio programme called *The Brains Trust* included the famous archaeologist Sir Mortimer Wheeler and in the great post-war programme of the Labour Party the protection of archaeological sites as part of our 'heritage' (a recent concept) was included in the Town and Country Planning Act and subsequent legislation. Rural West Cornwall's sites benefited too from this widening public and governmental interest.

Chun from the Air (Courtesy CES)

In 1961 the West Cornwall Field Club was transformed into the Cornwall Archaeological Society, with highly organised and skilled members. Their important ideas such as annual parish checklists, organised field-walking and the Sites and Monuments Register, as well as increasingly scientific excavations, were revealing more and more of Cornwall's ancient history.

At the same time the discipline of archaeology as an academic subject began to sub-divide amongst its increasing number of practitioners. In 1964 the concept of Industrial Archaeology was introduced

---

[76] Leeds: 205; Hencken

to the surprised members of the Cornwall Archaeological Society[77] who were accustomed to seeing mining as part of the scenery and nothing to do with archaeology. It was soon realised that it was very useful to be able to interview people who had worked in a vanishing industry and could actually explain the uses of the various ruins. The following decades, as the mining industry finally disappeared and the tourism industry increased, saw a growth in the co-operative work of historians and archaeologists which led in 2006 to the establishment of the West Cornwall mining areas as a World Heritage site.

Carn Euny from the Air (Courtesy CES)

An early sub-division of archaeology, which was to prove of particular relevance to West Cornwall, was that of Landscape Archaeology. This moves away from small, discrete sites and monuments to consider larger areas, anything from a farm to a region, and looks not only at current patterns on the landscape such as settlements, field boundaries, communications, and land use, but also at what patterns may be discerned from earlier periods and the processes by which one pattern may have changed into another. Its main tools are fieldwork, aerial photography and records, and there is necessarily close co-operation with historians and geologists. In the 1990s the county archaeologists of Cornwall piloted research into a method of landscape characterisation, financed by both local authorities and English Heritage. The Historic Landscape Character map produced is now widely consulted (see coloured illustration in centre of book). It maps those features on the landscape which are made by people, and it is gratifying that this type of mapping was pioneered in Cornwall and is now copied in other parts of the country. Considering the difficulties of interpreting West Penwith landscapes in particular, which have evolved over so many thousands of years, with so many generations using the same surface in so many different ways, it is a remarkable achievement.

Another recent specialism is the recognition that it may not be enough merely to list and describe human sites and artefacts; efforts should be made to identify the landscape as it was perceived by the people who lived on it at a particular time. Questions considered might be why barrows were built in certain locations—did they mark tribal boundaries, or reassure a community that their ancestors were looking after them from nearby? Another question considered has been how far people are affected by the physical and human landscape around them, or vice versa—how did they try to control their environment? A further development in this approach is found in the work of phenomenological archaeologists who try to interpret how the individuals of a past group may have seen the landscape in terms of their own memories and beliefs. Perhaps a Bronze Age woman always walked around a

---

[77] Cornish Archaeology no 3 *Industrial Archaeology in the South-West* (1964): 80-83

particular bush because she once saw a snake there; the kink she made in the village footpath became a permanent bend, still to be seen in the later Iron Age field-boundary and the much later modern road. The report on the Leskernick excavation on Bodmin Moor was one of the first examples of this approach[78] and has led to much debate. Whilst fairly sensible suggestions can be made about the utility and uses of physical objects and remains, evidence about how people saw their surroundings in ancient times may only be tentatively inferred, and then from the point of view of the modern archaeologist, itself a biased view.

However, as Caradoc Peters[79] has pointed out, whilst even at the start of the twenty-first century Cornish archaeologists may take account of the various current theoretical ideas, material evidence is still at the centre of any investigation. A recent excavation in the Scilly Isles provides a splendid example of the array of technological techniques now available for such evidence.

In this case[80] the site was a very small cist grave, about 2.25m long and just under 2m wide, found when a Bryher farmer's tractor wheel sank into it. He investigated and pulled out an ancient sword which, when he took it to the local museum, turned out to be a find of national importance: the first Iron Age sword found in Cornwall. Within a very short time, the Cornwall Archaeology Unit (now the Historic Environment Service of the County Council) had produced a project design, acquired English Heritage and the British Museum as partners and designated the site as a National Monument to protect it legally. Within six months, the excavation was under way and over a few weeks, on this very small site, the following techniques were used:-

magnetometer and resistivity surveys; three-dimensional recordings as the cist was excavated in spits (layers); sampling of 800 soil specimens using a grid pattern for each layer; measured drawings for each stage, transferred to computer; comparisons between objects and traces found with those of warrior graves over Britain; images from a scanning electron microscope on tiny bone fragments found; examination of teeth by experts to show age at death; DNA analysis on a small skull fragment (failed to establish sex); carbon and nitrogen stable isotope ratios calculated and comparisons made with other Iron Age materials from SW England (these showed that about a quarter of the dietary protein of the individual came from seafoods); x-rays of all metal finds so decorations could be seen and compared with others from all over Western Europe; electron microscopy to identify textile and animal fibres.

The surrounding land was also investigated with small excavations: another burial and an Iron Age Romano-British settlement site were found, with lynchets (ancient field terraces) in its fields. The all-important pottery fragments were given detailed petrographic descriptions and those of local origin were identified as well as those from imported pots, by the distinguished Cornishman Professor Charles Thomas. Every small bone found by sieving soil was analysed and tables drawn up showing the numbers of different species of birds, fish and mammals being consumed in the settlement. Many samples were taken for geoarchaeological and bioarchaeological analysis, including pollen analysis. Finally, perception was considered—i.e. a theory that such cists are intentionally boat-shaped and the possibility that the inclusion of a mirror in the grave indicated the occupant had been a wealthy woman, or alternatively, that the mirror had some magical and ritual significance.

The other major development in post-war archaeology, alongside these theoretical and technological changes, was the extension of the law protecting sites and monuments, and later, finds. In the Minutes of the various committees of Cornwall County Council there is no mention either of archaeology or ancient monuments until the run-up to the reorganisation of local government in 1974.[81] The Planning Department first discussed the employment of an Archaeological Officer in 1973. This officer would prepare proposals for the protection and enjoyment of Ancient Monuments and museums, and provide an input for the forthcoming Structure Plan. In the event, no appointment was made at that time and the Issues of Key Importance in the first Plan did not include archaeology. The Council was, however, providing some financial support to the Institute of Cornish Studies and to museums if applicants could show that they contributed to education in Cornish schools. Both the national and county council budgets in the 70s were tightly controlled in view of the oil crisis and serious balance-of-payments

---

[78] Bender: 147-178.
[79] Peters, Caradoc, *The Archaeology of Cornwall*, Fowey 2005
[80] Johns: 1-79.
[81] Index.

problems, so it is not surprising that archaeology came fairly low down on the list in allocating scarce resources. In 1976 the County did begin to take some responsibility for archaeology and a rescue service was started, with some emergency assessment and examination when a site was found, typically during building development.

By the end of the decade, largely due to the long period of work by Lady Aileen Fox, archaeology had grown to be a flourishing part of the Department of History at Exeter University, and in 1979 Malcolm Todd was appointed to the newly established Chair. As Cornwall's nearest university, this was encouraging for those wanting to develop the discipline professionally in the county. The last quarter of the twentieth century saw a continuous growth in public interest and awareness of archaeology in Cornwall, accompanied by a flow of legislation from central government, percolating down to local authorities and new organisations.

The first Act seeking to protect Ancient Monuments was as early as 1882, followed by the creation of the Royal Commissions on Ancient and Historic Monuments in 1908. Other legislation followed, mainly in the last half of the twentieth century, probably the most important being the Act of 1979. A few years later English National Heritage was created and the Act was amended in 2002 to extend the definition of an archaeological site to include the remains of vehicles, vessels, aircraft or other movable structures, when they are found on or under the seabed of our territorial waters. At the time of writing (2007) the Cornwall and Isles of Scilly Maritime Archaeology Society is undertaking a detailed survey of Mount's Bay, to record and survey all wrecks, as part of our maritime heritage. Also, after decades of mutual dislike and confrontation, archaeologists and metal detectorists are approaching peaceful co-existence through the Portable Antiquities Scheme (created by the Treasure Act 1996). The law is now clear on what should happen to small finds, and there is a great increase in the number of finds being reported. This is leading to enlarged databases and is already suggesting changes in earlier analyses of the movements and settlement patterns of prehistoric and medieval people. An example of co-operation in West Cornwall is that the County's Portable Antiquities officer attends the monthly meetings of the Kernow Search and Recovery Club at Hayle, helping members identify their finds, and of course, adding the details to the County's files. An Iron Age gold coin recently discovered at Crowlas was found in this way and was bought by the Royal Cornwall Museum.

Cornwall now has a fully professional Historic Environment Service, with a staff of about 35. It is widely consulted for planning advice and carries out early assessments of possible new sites found as land surfaces are disturbed for various reasons. If excavation is recommended, then the Service can submit bids, as do private contractors, and carry out the work if successful. The Service has recently played a key role in the achievement of World Heritage site status. Steve Hartgroves' aerial photography is revealing many new details of our ancient landscape. Much of the Service's daily work is concerned with providing information to the public and to educational bodies.

To summarise, this article has suggested some of the major developments in archaeology in West Cornwall, although clearly much detail has been omitted. Three aspects might be highlighted. Firstly, in the twentieth century, there has been a widening of interest in the ancient world amongst the general public and especially young people familiar with archaeology through popular television programmes such as Time Team and popular films about Indiana Jones! Although this can lead to some complaints from universities, who think applicants have an over-inflated view of the potential excitements of archaeology, most agree that a lively public interest in the subject cannot be a bad thing.

Secondly, increased legislation is going some way to care for those obvious—and also the invisible—sites and monuments which make West Cornwall such an important landscape. Some would argue that there is still much to be done. Private owners of land on which ancient features exist and which are not within the net of state protection can still remove or destroy them as the owners wish, but it is difficult to see how the law could be extended to provide complete protection.

Thirdly, the growth of technology has seen a major change in the possibilities of discovering and analysing ancient sites. It is now reaching a state where excavation, always destructive, is giving way to methods of 'seeing' what is below, for example by using ground-penetrating radar. Excavation will always be needed but less often, so that much remains hidden from view and damage, and is safe for future generations wanting to study the ancient past of West Cornwall.

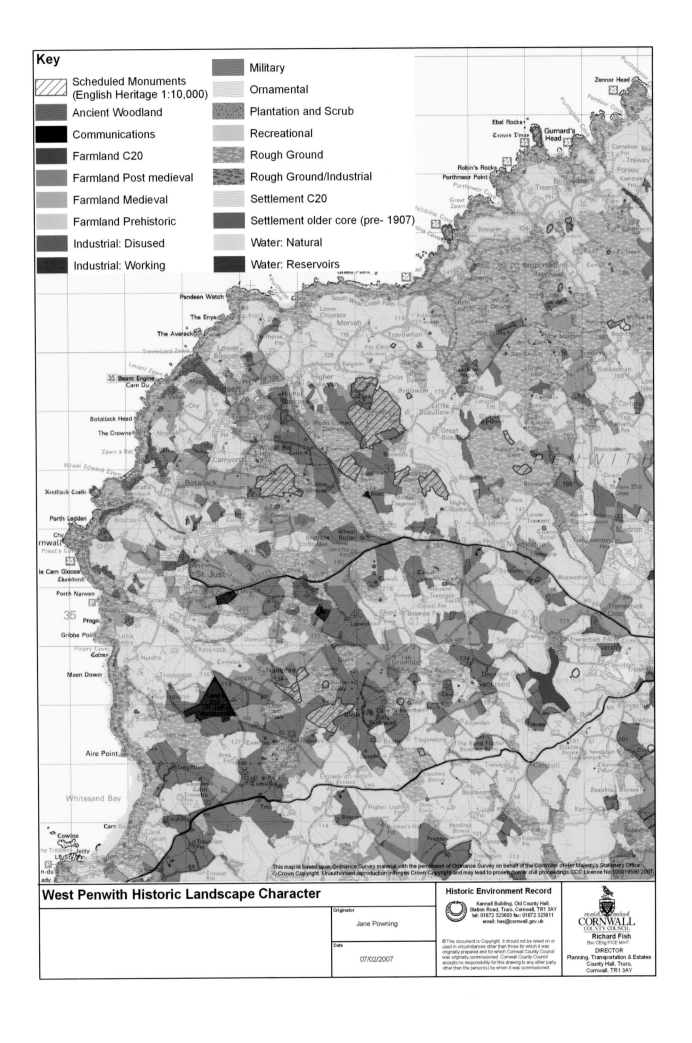

Key

Scheduled Monuments (English Heritage 1:10,000)		Military	
Ancient Woodland		Ornamental	
Communications		Plantation and Scrub	
Farmland C20		Recreational	
Farmland Post medieval		Rough Ground	
Farmland Medieval		Rough Ground/Industrial	
Farmland Prehistoric		Settlement C20	
Industrial: Disused		Settlement older core (pre- 1907)	
Industrial: Working		Water: Natural	
		Water: Reservoirs	

This map is based upon Ordnance Survey material with the permission of Ordnance Survey on behalf of the Controller of Her Majesty's Stationery Office © Crown Copyright. Unauthorised reproduction infringes Crown Copyright and may lead to prosecution or civil proceedings. CCC Licence No.100019590 2007

West Penwith Historic Landscape Character

Originator Jane Powning	
Date 07/02/2007	

Historic Environment Record

Kennall Building, Old County Hall, Station Road, Truro, Cornwall, TR1 3AY tel: 01872 323603 fax: 01872 323811 email: hes@cornwall.gov.uk

© This document is Copyright. It should not be relied on or used in circumstances other than those for which it was originally prepared and for which Cornwall County Council was originally commissioned. Cornwall County Council accepts no responsibility for this drawing to any other party other than the person(s) by whom it was commissioned.

CORNWALL COUNTY COUNCIL

Richard Fish Bsc CEng FICE MIHT DIRECTOR Planning, Transportation & Estates County Hall, Truro, Cornwall, TR1 3AY

Above: The sun is dipping in the west as Newlyn trawler Golden Spinney heads for the harbour with the accompanying seagulls (Photograph, Glyn Richards)

Below: Threshing corn at Trewey, Zennor, with a 1929 steam engine on 8 September 1996. Arthur Mann is in the white hat on the left. (Photograph, Jean Nankervis)

Above: 'Playing the Melodies' Grand Organ, a regular feature at Corpus-Christi Fairs in Penzance
(Photograph, Ann Altree)

Below: Wheal Betsy Cottage, an Arts and Craft house in Newlyn
(Photograph, Ron Hogg)

The "TRAVELOGUE" of

SILENT GUIDE PATENTED SERVICE

Knowtoring
SOMETHING MORE THAN MERELY MOTORING

Raising the curtain
on the
WESTERN NATIONAL COACH
TOURS FROM PENZANCE AND ST. IVES

ONE SHILLING

VOL. 4

8. Renouncing War: the Nancledra Community 1940-1947

Susan Hoyle

This is an account of a group of pacifists who worked a number of farms in Penwith in the early years of the Second World War. The Community did not remain here long: several of them moved to Constantine and stayed there until 1947; other key members had to move upcountry after only a couple of years, and that group, now called Taena, survives at Upton-St-Leonard's in Gloucestershire.[82] Most members were incomers who had made their homes here before the war began; although they had moved away by the war's end, their idea of West Cornwall remained an important expression of the ideal community they strove to create.

'Shelley's at the Door!'

In 1939, there was a glut of blue agricultural paint in the Nancledra area (on the back road between Penzance and St Ives), and somehow several farmhouse-doors came to be painted with it. Once the war began, the people then living behind those doors—who had had nothing to do with the decision to 'go blue'—came to the attention of the local police. One day in mid-1940, Connie Ineson was alone at Baldhu when they called 'and turned the place over.' They also asked her about a man on a blue-doored small-holding at nearby Amalebrea. She knew nothing about him, but her husband George went to visit him, and met Gerald Vaughan. A little later, the police knocked on the blue door at Castle Farm, and asked Bettina Stern whether she was a spy. At about the same time, George Ineson, attracted by the door, went up to Castle Farm to investigate. Anne Crockett (Bettina's sister) looked out of a window and, seeing the evidently charismatic figure of Ineson, called to her husband John: 'Shelley's at the door!' Thus began a lifelong friendship between the Inesons and the Crocketts, and also the Nancledra Community.[83]

The police thought the doors were a signal to enemy parachutists, but these people were not moles: they were pacifists, brought together by the police action. The Inesons, the Crocketts and Gerald Vaughan quickly formed a casual but defined group, and others joined them.

Contemporary Pacifism

In October 1934, Canon HRL (Dick) Sheppard had sent a letter to many local and national newspapers: it asked men to sign and send him a postcard saying 'I renounce war and never again, directly or indirectly, will I support or sanction another'. Six months later he had over 50,000 signatures. In 1936, this movement became the Peace Pledge Union (PPU), *Peace News* was launched, and women were allowed to sign as well as men. By 1937 membership was nearly 120,000, rising to a peak of 136,000 in spring 1940, with some 300 local groups, including one in Penzance. Most of the people who would join the Nancledra Community were members.

Penzance was a thriving branch, attracting leading pacifist speakers: for example, Donald Soper spoke at St John's Hall in April 1938. Of course, not everyone supported their stance: a week later, a *Cornishman* editorial branded the pacifists as 'disloyal'; other editorials upheld the democratic right of pacifists and other 'practised controversialists' to free speech, but at the same time declined to allow them much, if any, space in the paper, especially once the war began.[84]

On the day war was declared, 3 September 1939, every male in the United Kingdom aged between 18 and 40 became liable for conscription under the new National Service (Armed Forces) Act.[85] Because the First World War had been the first in the UK to use full-time mass conscription, it had brought the state up against conscientious objection as never before, and its response came to be generally regarded as excessive if not brutal. By 1939 it was agreed at the highest levels that the next time the matter would be handled more sensitively. 'It was a useless and exasperating effort to attempt to force such people to act in a manner contrary to their principles,' said the Prime Minister, Neville

---

[82] Utopia. For full bibliographical details, see the Bibliography on pp. 113-116.

[83] PB and AC; Ineson (1956): 31, 34.

[84] *The Cornishman and Cornish Telegraph*, 6 April 1938: 3; 13 April 1938 (2nd edition); 20 April 1938 (2nd edition,) p. 5; 27 April, 1938, p. 7; 4 May 1938.

[85] In late 1941, the age-limit for men was raised to 51. National Service (Armed Forces) Act 1939 (2 & 3 Geo VI) c 81; National Service (No 2) Act 1941 (5 & 6 Geo VI) c4.

Chamberlain, of his own experience on a CO Tribunal during the Great War. This time, if the principles were 'conscientiously held, we desire that they should be respected, and that there should be no persecution.'[86] Not every Tribunal member in World War II felt the same, but the treatment of objectors was less harsh than before.

Perhaps because of this, but certainly because of the still vivid memories of the slaughter in the trenches of 1914-18, nearly four times as many men claimed exemption this time (c60,000) and only half as many went to gaol (c3,000). Another 3,000 were given unconditional exemption, many of them Quakers; some 18,000 claims were regarded as not genuine; and the remainder (almost 40,000 people) were either given conditional exemption, which meant being employed on agreed civilian work, or were registered as non-combatants with the military.[87]

'Agreed civilian work' was often farming, but contrary to the popular impression, farming was not a reserved occupation, and people engaged in it were not exempt. It was a restricted occupation, in that if you were employed in farming you needed permission from the Employment Exchange to move to other work, but neither the Employment Exchange nor the Tribunals ever made difficulties about men leaving the land to fight, and they were not impressed simply by a man's having got himself an agricultural job as part of his CO case, especially if he were under 30.[88] Another misconception is that conscientious objectors were all pacifists. Most were, but for example, some British fascists registered as conscientious objectors, their objection being not to war, but to war against Nazi Germany.[89] However, all the men in the Nancledra Community were certainly pacifists and the women too. Many people did not understand the distinction, however, and there was a common perception that pacifists were 'on Hitler's side'.

One study has detected three types of pacifist response to war: 'relief, resistance and reconstruction'. Agricultural communities (such as Nancledra) set out to achieve reconstruction:

[which] emphasizes the role of pacifists as a redemptive minority, bearing witness to a higher order of morality and pointing the way towards a new order of communal life ... [For them,] the true role of the pacifist in wartime was that of planting the seeds of a new civilization within the barbarism and insanity of a world bent on destruction.[90]

The *Community Broadsheet* (1940-46) was published nationally by the Community Service Committee to help, encourage and advise such groups. The prototypical community was the Adelphi Centre, set up by the well known writer John Middleton Murry in 1934 in Langham, Essex. After war broke out, there were many others (e.g. the Holton Beckering Community Land Training Association in Lincolnshire and the Kingston Community at Charney Bassett near Wantage), but the only one I know of in Cornwall was based at Nancledra. (There were other pacifists, but no other pacifist agricultural community.)

Pacifists themselves notoriously fail to agree on what constitutes pacifism. Some will work with the armed forces as non-combatants; others refuse to do anything which assists the war-effort; still others simply refuse to acknowledge the right of the state to direct their activities at all; and there are various positions in between. The line the British government took was to respect the individual conscience, once it was satisfied that that conscience was genuinely offended by the war—a difficult matter, but establishing it was the nub of the tribunals' task.

Cornwall COs came under the South Western tribunal, which was based at Bristol.[91] Sadly none of the tribunal papers for Cornwall (or anywhere else) has survived, but the Central Board for Conscientious Objectors (CBCO) kept track of events at the time, and its archives are an invaluable resource. It advised COs on how to handle their tribunals and appeals, and kept records of the correspondence; and there are many boxes of press-cuttings. In the CBCO *Bulletin*, it published all the statistics it could muster, and also very objective accounts of the chief concerns of both COs and those dealing with them on behalf of the state, covering both specific cases and also the general legal and moral issues which those cases raised. It is thus possible to piece together something of the picture in

---

[86] Quoted at PPU COB.

[87] PPU COB.

[88] Thanks to WH for explaining this to me.

[89] Griffiths. Sir Oswald Mosley later lied about giving this advice to his members.

[90] Rigby, quoted in Makin: 3.

[91] The Tribunal did convene elsewhere from time to time, and it may have come to Truro. WH, 1 March 2007.

the South-West as compared with the rest of Britain—though not of Cornwall, let alone Penwith. The statistics show that the South-West had an exceptional level of appeals: it granted unconditional exemptions fifteen times more often than their London colleagues, for example, and refused CO status relatively seldom. Nearly all tribunals became less generous over time, and fewer COs came forward, but the South-West remained relatively busier and more tolerant. A 1942 CBCO analysis of appellate decisions reported that 'the South-Western Tribunal in its worst period was more generous than the North-Western in its best period'—and the North-Western's worst was better than London's best.[92] What is not at all clear is *why* there was this marked regional variation.

Overall there is evidence that tribunals everywhere were less impressed by political than religious opposition to war. A judge's remark that true conscientious objection was religious and not disloyal, found many echoes amongst tribunal chairmen.[93] But there is also evidence that religious objection was either more common, or more commonly claimed: there is an impression that the best argument a CO could advance was a letter from a clergyman saying that while the cleric did not share X's views, he was convinced of his sincerity. Some tribunals were very hostile to political objections—one chairman said they lacked true Christian humility—and so some people may have framed their claims accordingly.

The Nancledra Community[94]

The men who later joined the Nancledra Community were nearly all in their early to mid-twenties when the war began. **John Crockett** (21) had to register at his local Employment Exchange (the first stage in the process) on 3 June 1939, and again 21 October 1939; **Gerald Vaughan** (24) and **Sid Watson** (also 24) had to register 9 March 1940, and **George Ineson** (25) on Saturday 6 April 1940.[95] Their Tribunals were eight to twelve weeks later. None of them had religious grounds for their stand, but all except Sid Watson appear to have received a B decision (i.e. civilian work under civilian control—which in their case meant farming). On 19 November 1940, Sid Watson appealed against his initial rating—which since his objection was to carrying a rifle must have been D—and gained a B.[96]

Who were these men (and their families)? For a start, they were not alone: 'Already by the summer of 1940, wherever land was neglected, sodden or sterile enough to be cheap, groups of young men and women, as liberally endowed with energy and idealism as they were deficient in funds and experience, were diligently establishing 'new patterns of living'.[97] In this spirit, in September 1940, a year after the Second World War began, our group set up as an agricultural co-operative in some farms around Nancledra. Only George Ineson called it the Nancledra Community, nor has anyone else referred to it as more than a loose-knit group.[98]

George Hudswell Ineson (1914-1995), the driving force behind the group, its resident intellectual, and its leader, was very attractive to women, and had a strong need for vivid experience. Although he was not always easy to get on with, no one seems to have resented his pre-eminence.[99] Having early lost the Methodist faith in which he had been brought up, he had become involved in socialist and anarchist politics and, shortly after it was founded, with the PPU. In late 1935 he met Connie Groves, a fellow pacifist, who became his wife. He qualified as an architect at Easter 1937, and was already discussing setting up a rural community on the edges of London.[100] By late 1938 he had landed a job in an architect's office in Penzance (possibly with Cowell, Drewitt and Wheatley in Lloyds Bank Chambers), designing the new elementary school at either Treneere or Newlyn; later he also worked

---

[92] Faulkner: 6-7.

[93] Newell vs Gillingham reported in *CBCO Bulletin*, March 1941.

[94] The information about the farms, unless otherwise stated, is from the NFS A and *CB*, Jan-May 1942: 23. Personal information was provided by JPV and PB, and by Ineson (1956).

[95] WH calculated these dates for me.

[96] William Sydney Watson: Appellate card: appeal against SW local tribunal 19 Nov 1940; CBCO archive. Thanks to Josef Keith for this item. The Tribunal code was A: unconditional exemption; B: civilian work under civilian control; C: non-combatant duties in the Forces; D: liable for military service

[97] Lea: 292, quoted by Makin: 1.

[98] *CB*, Jan-May 1942: 23.

[99] AC; PB.

[100] Ineson: 1-26.

(with Geoffrey Bazeley in the Greenmarket) on a new girls' school (possibly what is now Penwith College).[101]

My first weeks in Cornwall were vivid with the joy of liberation; the bicycle ride each day to work along the coast, the sea and the wind, the fishing boats and the people, were like food to a starving body...Everywhere the sound of seagulls crying, the stories of the wind after its lonely flight across the Atlantic, the living marks of an elemental culture reaching backwards to the past—downwards and inwards to the roots of our nature.[102]

This theme, more or less romantic, of Penwith as a theatre of unique opportunity (for incomers if not for those born here) is familiar in twentieth-century history: George Ineson was not alone in his exhilaration, nor in his decision to make his unconventional home here. He responded to 'a generosity which assumed that you took anyone into your home if they were in difficulties, a despising of material possessions and power over others'. He was true to those ideals to the end of his life, although he learned very different ways of explaining their importance and effect.

Not long after the war began, George's job at the architect's office ended and by the summer of 1940 he, Connie, Connie's mother and (from May 1941) their daughter Ruth rented a cottage at Baldhu in Nancledra. He had been directed to farmwork by his Tribunal and, 'unused to continuous physical work,' would come home 'in a state of collapse'. They had a scant 1½ acres where they kept a couple of goats for themselves, and grew beans, lettuce, and early potatoes, presumably mainly for sale. George had charge of a two-wheeled BMB tractor of the sort made for market gardens. He not only travelled round the Community's farms doing the ploughing and cultivating, he also undertook some contract ploughing for local farmers.

The Inesons were still 'desperate' to start a community.[103] George wrote: 'I began to discuss with other pacifists of the district ways and means of earning a living'. It is important to remember that answering the question of how to earn a decent living—'decent' not just as in 'adequate', but far more importantly as in 'morally and socially justifiable'—was the very essence of what this group was about—this group and many others. It was at this time, early 1941 that the blue doors played their trick, and the Nancledra Community came into being.

It was the independently wealthy **Thomas Francis Gerald Vaughan** (1915-1984) who provided the cash—and much of the farming expertise. He was only briefly a member of the Community, but it would not have survived its first few months without him, let alone its later crises. He was named after Gerald Du Maurier, whose manager was his father, Tom Benjamin Vaughan—a self-made man. Both Gerald's parents were dead by the time he was 13, a tragedy which set the tone for much of the rest of his life. Fast-forwarding to the middle of 1938, we find Gerald, his wife Ellaline, and their five-month-old son Patrick moving to the community of the Society of Brothers. The Bruderhof, as it was called, was a communal, pacifist sect; they had left Hitler's Germany in 1934, and by 1936 were in Wiltshire. Gerald made over most of his inheritance to them, perhaps as much as £20,000,[104] but they asked him to leave not long afterwards. Meanwhile, Ellaline Vaughan had become seriously ill, which eventually led to her commitment to St Lawrence's, Bodmin, for the rest of her life. Gerald and his baby son had to cope without her: they came to Newlyn, bringing with them a young Jewish-German refugee, Ingeborg Mendelsohn (b 1921). What peace they may have had there was shattered when Inge was taken into custody in early 1940 as an enemy alien; she was detained on the Isle of Man until 1943. The next blow was when Gerald heard that his only brother was dead: Lt John Gilbert Vaughan of the Fleet Air Arm was killed on the last day of August 1940, aged 21.

Thus Gerald came into the rest of his father's money, and proceeded to give most of that away too. He had by now moved to Amalebrea Hill, just outside Nancledra. (The locals called the direction 'up

---

[101] Ineson: 26-27 refers to working on an elementary school: the *Cornishman* of 17 August 1938 reports that Messrs Cowell, Drewitt and Wheatley were appointed by the Council as architects for these schools. For the Bazeley contract, see *Architects' Journal* 1940.

[102] Ineson: 26-27, 31.

[103] Ineson: 31; PB.

[104] Tom Vaughan left nearly £43,000 in 1928, in trust to his 'infant sons' in equal shares; the calculator at http://www.measuringworth.com translates £20,000 to £5,326,124.94 in 2005 money using the GDP. Billingham: 94, asserts that the Vaughan fortune was based on 'the global tobacco industry', but he obviously confused the connexion with Gerald Du Maurier with the cigarette brand.

windy'.) Gerald Vaughan was here first, then Maurice Frost and his family came (until he had to leave under doctor's orders), and finally the Crocketts moved in. Table 1 gives some idea of the place, although it is data from the Crocketts' time.

As described, the mysterious affair of the blue doors led the Inesons to him. Gerald was not a member of the Penzance PPU, and does not seem at that stage to have had strong political interests (as opposed to social). George's romantic socialist vision of community perhaps reminded Gerald too much of what he had seen at the Bruderhof; perhaps it offended his secular approach to life. Pip Walker (from Newlyn, who became his partner) remembers Gerald thinking that George and company were 'a bunch of bloody amateurs:' even though Gerald himself was also new to farming, he took it much more seriously. He eventually bought several farms in the wider district, and elsewhere. For example he purchased farms for the Holton Beckering community: in mid 1941 he gave them Holton Grange rent-free for seven years, thus doubling the number of trainees they could take to twenty.[105]

It is worth considering Holton Beckering in distant Lincolnshire because of Gerald Vaughan's evident interest in and support for its activities and aims. Trainees usually stayed there for a year, learning basic farming skills and building their strength and stamina.[106] This may well be how Vaughan had hoped that Nancledra would develop—and might explain why he withdrew early on from day-to-day involvement with Ineson's dream, which was not so much about training people as about creating a utopian community.

Here is George's later account of their beginnings in farming:

> *The early days of learning to milk, to plough with horses, to make hay and reap the corn, were unforgettable. We had no money to buy much in the way of implements and, as a result, we were learning the feel of the earth directly and intimately, scything the corn and binding by hand, planting and lifting the potatoes with the long-handled Cornish shovel. We had meetings now and again but no form of authority or discipline; we very soon met difficulties in personal relationships and discovered that we had no knowledge at all of how to deal with them.[107]*

As things became more settled: 'We became very fond of Jimmy, the pony, who not only ploughed, cultivated and carted for us, but once a week took us into Penzance to sell vegetables and eggs, collect waste food for the pigs, and do the shopping.'[108] This was what any other farming family would have done in those years. What was different was how the economy of the Community evolved:

> *Our main income was from milk production, but we also kept pigs, poultry and goats, and grew vegetables for sale. In the beginning we just shared the income—which was about £1 per week for a married couple; but later on we decided that this was unfair, as some of us had occasional gifts of money from outside. We therefore agreed to pool all our income and possessions, but as we were then living in five separate houses it was not possible to do more than accept it as a principle and do what we could to even things out.[109]*

It was at this point that Gerald Vaughan left. George Ineson says that it was because he thought that it was 'not possible to live in community without a shared religious faith'[110]—which they (including Vaughan) did not have. Deleting 'religious' from the comment probably makes more sense of it, as Vaughan was and remained a

John Crockett & family, 1942						Total acreage					Cattle			Livestock		Fowl		
Cond'n		Rating	Water	Elec'y			Arable	Croft	Fodder	For sale	Corn	Cows	Bull	Calves	Pigs	Goats	Chickens	Other	Horses
Bldgs	Land																		
Bad	Fair	B	roof	no		66	11¼		2	¾	2	3	3		11	5	85	7	3
Comments: lack of capital of experience, a poor holding situated at a high altitude.																		

Table 1
Amalebra Hill and Trenowan Downs (Nancledra)

---

[105] *CB*, Summer–Autumn 1941: 31. See also Murry.

[106] Victor Farley, the accountant of the Community Farming Society Limited, writing in *CB*, Autumn–Winter 1942: 20. There was a programme about this group on BBC R4, *The Conchies of Holton-cum-Beckering* (broadcast 7 May 2007).

[107] Ineson: 32-33.

[108] Ineson: 35.

[109] Ineson: 34, 35.

[110] Ineson: 35.

very secular man, chary of organized religion. He wanted to farm, and to use his money to help other pacifists to farm. He found the late-night discussions at Baldhu about the politics of community and about the principles on which they should decide how to act an almost complete waste of time. Farmers should not stay up late jawing: they had real work to do in the morning.[111]

Vaughan left, and the Crocketts moved from Castle Farm into Amalebrea Hill. **John Crockett** (1918-1986) was an artist and his wife Anne (née Stern, b 1918) had trained as a dancer. A friend recalled John's attitude thus:

He was in violent revolt against his father's military tradition; his father was a regular army officer... [John] was so possessed by waves of inarticulate rage against the world in general and especially his own upbringing that he seemed like those figures in the Gospels who fall to the ground incapable ... before Jesus drives the devil out of them.[112]

His wife says that all he wanted to do was to paint, but by spring 1941 if not earlier, they were in the house with a blue door at Castle Farm. Very shortly afterwards George Ineson met him, and by that summer, the Crockett household (John, Anne and her sister Bettina) had joined the Community. Castle Farm (which no longer exists as a separate farm) was near Castle-an-Dinas, up the hill from Nancledra towards Penzance. There were five and a half acres of arable and about sixty acres of rough croft. Their main crop was cattle fodder, plus half an acre of parsnips for sale; they also had three milking cows, three heifers, a pony, two pigs, six goats, as well as ducks, geese, fowls and bees. It looks as though the Inesons worked this farm after the Crocketts had gone to Amalebrea Hill, as George speaks of giving up the lease on it at the same time as Amalebrea Hill and Baldhu.[113]

Vaughan left, but he made sure that his going did not damage the group. He 'very generously [left] behind him an interest-free loan and two farms near Constantine'.[114] The Watsons and the Wilkinsons took on these farms, while the Inesons and Crocketts remained around Nancledra.

William Sydney Watson (Sid, 1915-1998) and his wife Mabel (Mollie, 1911-96) were different from the other tyro farmers in this group: they were local and working class. Mollie was born in Penzance in 1911, one of six children of Ernest Lawrence of Ludgvan and Mabel Wright of Penzance. She had won a place at Penzance Art School but had to stay at home and help with the younger children. In the 1930s, she worked in the Penzance Trueform shoe-shop.[115] She married Sid in April 1937, and they bought themselves a house in Parc Letta, Heamoor, newly built on land owned by the Bolithos of Trengwainton.

Sid was born at Trevarth, Lanner, in 1915, and moved to Penzance in 1929, when his father, WCD Watson (1886-1959), became Head Gardener at the Morrab Gardens. Willie Watson was born in Mylor: a former Quaker, he was also a self-taught, ground-breaking scholar of Cornish, an early member of the Cornish Gorsedd, and even before that one of the first Cornish Bards (created in 1928, taking the name Tyrvab: Son of the Soil). Remarkable man though he was, he was never close to his family. There is no evidence, for example, that Willie's early Quakerism influenced Sid's pacifism.

Sid and Mollie were members of the Penzance PPU, where they probably met the Inesons: Sid was a founder member of the community in September 1940, although at that time he still had his pre-war job. (He was a house-painter and decorator for most of his working life, employed by Bob Rowe, the builder.) He cycled to Nancledra in the evening after a hard day's work. After he won his Tribunal appeal, he joined the community full-time. As the tensions in the group developed, Sid's attitude sounds very like Gerald's:

Dad would always have been at the practical end of a spectrum—trying something in theory was not his bag. He had a strong feel for nurturing land to be productive—he was horrified by ... burning straw stubble, it should always be ploughed back to give back the land's natural fertility.[116]

---

[111] JPV and PB.

[112] Billingham: 90, quoting Dellar: 4, quoting the poet Charles Brasch (1909-73).

[113] Ineson (1956): 35.

[114] *CB,* January-May 1942: 23.

[115] SEG.

[116] SEG.

Like Gerald, Sid wanted to farm. They loaned the Parc Letta house to Mollie's parents for the duration, and about a year later he and Mollie were installed at Little Treglidgwith, which was owned by Gerald Vaughan and worked by them rent-free.

At the farm there was no running water, electricity or gas. Water had to be drawn up from a well in the lane, meals were cooked and water heated on the Cornish slab, and light came from oil lamps. The ploughing was done by a horse called Queenie. The cows were named after [Mollie]'s sisters.[117]

Their daughter, Susan, was born at Treglidgwith in February 1945. Also living with them, weekends only, was 'Uncle', as he was always known, even outside the family. He was Sid's maternal uncle, Wesley Rogers (1886-1971), a road labourer who went back with them to Parc Letta in 1947 and lived there until his death, becoming a well known figure in Heamoor.

Little Treglidgwith is just north-east of Constantine—and thus not in Penwith. Table 2 summarizes the National Farm Survey findings. George Ineson considered Little Treglidgwith 'a difficult place to work—one field we ploughed this year had a slope of 1 in 2 ... However, it's beginning to look up as a result of much hard work.' The MAF official did not agree: he rated the farm B and gave as his reason (which he gave in other cases too): 'Lack of ambition'.

There were other people active in this group about whom I have discovered much less: **Maurice Frost**, briefly at Amalebrea Hill; **Geoffrey Pearson**, who was living and working at Little Treglidgwith in 1942, and **Ged Wilkinson** and his wife Millie, who farmed near the Watsons at Higher Carvedrass, another farm owned by Gerald Vaughan; they later moved to Perranporth. **Harold Bounden** (Harry) of Newlyn generally helped out, latterly with the Wilkinsons. George Ineson describes him as 'an ex-fish porter about 50 years old [who] goes home for week-ends. Position obviously a little difficult—but he is one of our most valued and cheerful members.'[118]

The end of the Nancledra community

Very soon after Gerald Vaughan left, it became obvious that the Penwith set needed more and better land (not least because the Employment Exchange did not regard their farms as viable), and that it would be sensible to move to be near the others at Constantine. Negotiations were well-advanced for them to take on the tenancy of a 40-acre holding at Michaelmas 1942,[119] when suddenly the landlord pulled out. It is likely that he did not want to let his land to pacifists, and it was a major blow. The Inesons and Crocketts had already given notice on their Nancledra leases, and would be homeless if they failed to find another property soon. John Crockett went up to London to see whether Middleton Murry and the Adelphi Centre could help them, but nothing could be done. At the last moment they accepted shelter from a small group at Ross-on-Wye.

Thus the Nancledra Community was split: the Constantine section remained in place until 1947; the Nancledra group went on to found Taena, which still exists. **Harry Bounden** seems to have been stranded when the Nancledra Community broke up: 'It was with sad hearts that we saw Harry sling his bag over his back and walk off over the hill; he had his home in Newlyn and it had seemed impracticable to leave it for a very uncertain future with us.'[120]

On the train leaving Penzance with the Inesons were the **Crocketts**. They all wondered how they could have brought themselves to do such a thing. George wrote: 'The only clue was a conversation I had had with John, which has remained vaguely in my memory: we were both so fond of Cornwall that we felt that unless we left now, we would remain there for the rest of our lives, lost in the twilight mist, held by the primeval siren voices.'[121]

There was a difficult interlude before they all found a base, during which John and Anne founded the influential Compass Players, but they, and the Players, eventually joined the Inesons at Taena.[122] They became Catholics like the Inesons, and retained close links with the community. John went on to

---

[117] SEG. The cows would therefore have been called Elizabeth, Mary, Winnie and Barbara.

[118] *CB,* Jan-May 1942: 23.

[119] I have been unable to find which farm it was.

[120] Ineson: 36. Harry's son Douglas still lives at Taena.

[121] Ineson: 37.

[122] The Players survived until 1952, when an Arts Council grant arrived just too late to save it from collapse.

Sid and Mollie Watson

Cond'n		Rating	Water	Elec'y	Total acreage		Fodder	For sale	Corn	Cattle			Pigs	Goats	Fowl		Horses
Bldgs	Land				Arable	Croft				Cows	Bull	Calves			Chickens	Other	
Good	Fair	B	well	no	11½	-	4½	¾	1	3							1

Comments: Lack of ambition; infestation of rooks and pigeons, hilly and rocky

Table 2

Little Treglidgwith (Constantine)

a career as an artist (and also to work on early *Dr Who* series!), and there was a major retrospective of his work at the Westminster Cathedral Gallery following his death in 1986. Anne Crockett lives in Newlyn now.

Gerald Vaughan left Nancledra, but did not go far: he had his own farm at Leswidden in St Just, where he stayed with Pip and Patta until 1946. Pip's three children with Gerald were born there, and Gerald's links to Holton Beckering continued: a couple of years later, the training farm was oversubscribed, and so Leswidden took on some of their young COs to teach them an early version of organic smallholding. **Pip Walker** (born in Newlyn in 1921) introduced Gerald to her kind of anarchism—they shared a 'distrust of the powers that be' and also an impatience with George Ineson's approach to farming. After the war, Gerald returned to London and edited *Freedom,* the anarchist newspaper, for some years. In 1947, he sold the Constantine farms, which were no longer viable, in an amicable arrangement with his tenants, who had to leave. He met **Inge Mendelsohn** again, and in 1949 they married; by 1953, Gerald was bankrupt. Sadly Inge was unable to have children; after her early death, Gerald was increasingly dependent upon alcohol. He died in 1984, at Taena. Pip went on to a career as an artist, illustrator and photographer. Together with her husband Asa Benveniste and her son Paul Vaughan, she set up the Trigram Press in 1965, using their own private printing presses. She lives in Dorset.

George and Connie Ineson separated for a few years, but then came together again. At Taena they discovered first Jung and then Roman Catholicism; George became a star in the English Catholic world, and wrote his autobiographical *Community Journey* about how he came to find faith and peace. He died at Taena in 1995.

Sid and Mollie Watson returned to Heamoor in 1947, and Sid took up his old job as a house-painter and decorator. He was responsible for the painting of the Egyptian House in Chapel Street, Penzance, when it was restored by the Landmark Trust in the 1970s, and he supervised the repainting in the 80s. After he retired he moved to Tregony to live with his son, Roger. Sue recalls that Sid:

...was an original thinker, able to formulate his own perspective on events. He was a regular contributor to phone in programmes on Radio Cornwall in the late 1980s, known as 'Sid of Tregony'. He could be argumentative, but had a great sense of humour and an endless supply of corny jokes.

The Watsons certainly remembered Vaughan with great fondness. It was from Sue Griffin, who was born at Little Treglidgwith that I first heard of Gerald Vaughan, and of his extraordinary generosity. Until I found the links in the research which I started at her request, she had hardly heard of George Ineson. Her parents had scarcely mentioned him.

Sid Watson with his daughter Susan at Little Treglidgwith in early 1947

(Courtesy Sue Griffin)

9. A Woman's Place? Madron Village Life 1918-1958

Jenny Dearlove

Madron Women's Institute [Madron WI] was founded in 1918 and changed local country women's lives.[123] It has the distinction of being the first institute to be set up in Cornwall, beating St Just WI by half a day. From 1914 women had been making strides towards greater participation in the outside world, and away from an exclusively domestic life where their kitchen duties alone included baking, brewing, curing fresh meat, and the gathering of herbs for home-made remedies.[124] Women aged 30 and over got the vote in 1918; the first woman Member of Parliament (Nancy Astor) was elected in 1919; women of 21 and over could vote on equal terms with men in 1928; Marie Stopes' first birth-control clinic was set up, for married couples only, in 1922; and women were granted equality in divorce litigation in 1923. In Penzance Mrs TR Bolitho was appointed first woman magistrate in 1920; and the first 'Lady Councillors' were elected to the Town Council in 1929.[125]

The WI movement is fundamentally democratic, non-sectarian, and non-party-political while membership is inclusive, being open to women of all ages, all classes, single or married.[126] With this in mind, annual subscriptions were kept at 2s from 1920 to 1943.[127] Of central importance are the social policy resolutions which any institute can put forward every year; selected resolutions are debated at the National Federation of Women's Institutes' (NFWI) annual general meeting in London, where one or two are chosen as mandates to campaign for legislative change. By 1918, when they had become independent of the Board of Agriculture, and their aims had broadened to include combating rural isolation and promoting women's right to leisure, it was already clear that members also wanted to have a good time together.

Madron Daniel school group circa 1916; the first generation to grow up in a Cornwall with WI opportunities
(Madron WI 'The story of our school')

---

[123] The Women's Institute Movement was started in Ontario, Canada, in 1897 and was founded in Britain in 1915; by 1917 it had become the responsibility of the Board of Agriculture. Launched with the aim of improving standards in food production and preparation, and encouraging community service, individual institutes were to be based in rural areas with a population of less than ten thousand people. (Donnelly: 10.) Towns with populations over 4,000 were permitted to form institutes in 1965.
[124] Martin.
[125] Saundry: 43-44.
[126] Andrews: xiii, 9-11; Jenkins: 11.
[127] Today it stands at £22.

While some women found fulfilment in a purely domestic role, many did not, as the success of the WI movement demonstrated. By sampling records in the years following 1918 and by the use of taped memories, I hope to show that Madron WI helped its members to emerge with increasing confidence from the traditional cycle of household drudgery and isolation, into the wider world of expanding opportunities; and that their tremendous organising skills (explicitly encouraged and developed by their participation in WI activities) had a markedly beneficial effect on village life.

Madron between the wars

The 1921 County Report taken from the census shows a total village population for Madron Urban District of 3,277. Of the 1,509 women and girls of working age (that is to say twelve years and over), only 395 were listed as employed, and they were working principally as maids, dressmakers, shop assistants and agricultural workers. Many women did seasonal work on the daffodil farms.

Daffodil picking in West Cornwall, 1936.
(Morrab Library collection)

The Cornishman in January 1918 offered fourteen jobs for women of which thirteen were domestic service of one kind or another and this pattern persisted up to 1938 at least.[128] With so many more women than men living in the area, a large number of women were not going to get married and would have expected to go out to work all their lives. However anyone, married or single, who could afford to stay at home did so because household tasks in rural Cornwall were so onerous, as can be inferred from Carlene Harry's grandfather's tale (chapter 3) and Jean Nankervis' Old Codgers (chapter 5).

These harsh home conditions and women's expected role in the family were feelingly expressed by Mrs Wilmay Le Grice of Trereife country house and estate:

Women's life was nothing but hard work. From the time they were little girls of eleven and twelve came the realisation that the man was the important part of their lives; from the age of about twelve and onwards it was the men that had to be catered for, the men had to have their meal on the table when they came back from work; it was all orientated towards men. Little

---

[128] The *Cornishman*, 3 Jan 1918; 12 Jan 1928; 1 Jan 1938.

girls from the age of eleven or twelve had to work because all the big commodities of their lives had to be fetched or carried or lifted or something, and so these small girls had to go out with the pails to the pump, and they had to go and fetch in wood for the fire, and almost all everyday things were done by women or young girls...And the floors of all their houses were really mostly sand on top of beaten earth; and so many babies [because] again the men had what they wanted. They didn't care that there were eleven children who needed to be fed and looked after. Very hard; and of course the workhouse was hanging over everybody's head.[129]

One lady born in Madron in 1915 recalled life without piped water, or birth control:

Sunday nights we had to fill up the bath and the boiler and all on the slab for washing next day. You had to carry all the water, you see. I know Mother would be washing in the morning when we go to school and four o'clock she was still doing the last socks; always used to leave the socks till last. Well she had fifteen children, you see.[130]

Some housewives still used to do the family laundry in the stream and dry it on the furze bushes in the traditional manner. The disposal of sewage was another problem: 'Some had bucket lavatories. We used to put ashes in the bucket as well, then they used to have a special thing come round and we'd dump it in. It was removed separate from the rubbish. It was the same at school, we only had bucket lavatories at school.'[131] Clean drinking water was not available at Madron Daniel Primary School in the 1920s, where

there was a stream which ran down along beside the school. We lay down and drank out of that. Of course it was always best to be first in the row because the water was cleaner. (After using the toilets) we washed our hands in the stream, the same stream we drank from, but nobody worried about that![132]

From oral accounts, employment appears mainly to have been offered by the Lord Lieutenant and Mrs Bolitho of Trengwainton House. One lady counted the number of servants working there in the 1920s:

I was born 1909. In Trengwainton when I was there, we were three in the kitchen; there was the cook, I was kitchen maid, and there was a scullery man. And then there was three housemaids: the head housemaid, the second housemaid and the third housemaid. The housemaid works upstairs, see, and the kitchen people were downstairs, in the great big kitchen; and then there was the butler and the parlour-maid...(On the farms) they probably used to have a dozen men, and people working in the gardens.[133]

Another lady remembers that her mother used to leave her alone at home to go out to milk:

I was about 3 year old; she used to give me a biscuit and a drop to drink, pull back the curtain and a few crumbs put out on the walls for me to watch the birds, and Mother used to go out Landithy (a farm on the Bolitho estate) and milk the cows. Cos they never used to bring the men in from the fields to do the milking. Mother used to milk about fourteen cows morning and evening, by hand.[134]

It was agreed by a group of current members how the hard conditions affected their mothers and grandmothers; they 'looked older then; they were old-looking when they were middle-aged; they dressed older too.'[135] These were the lives that the WI changed when it came to the village in 1918.

Madron WI had every reason to be proud of their first year's programme which included:

- <u>demonstrations, classes and talks</u> on fruit-bottling, laundry, the work of the Red Cross with a film, shoe mending, cheese making, garden and allotment work, dress-making and knitting

- entertainment : 'Mr Creek to be asked to sing', recitations, lantern slides, Cornish stories

---

[129] Le Grice tape.
[130] Starnes: 1.
[131] Starnes: 1.
[132] Madron WI: 93
[133] Starnes: 3.
[134] Starnes: 1.
[135] Madron WI meeting.

- cup of tea and a bite to eat: this would have included some of the dishes later printed in Edith Martin's 1929 Cornish Recipes, such as splits, heavy cake, figgie hobbin, and muggity pie; Madron WI contributed recipes for fuggan, roast bream and metheglin to this publication.[136]

- activities: a pig club—this was a big undertaking in which all members could buy a share at one shilling; two members were to feed the pig and it was intended that the Girl Guides collect the manure (though I think this offer was declined); Mrs E.'s husband was to kill the pig and Mrs P.'s daughter was to sell the pork. Each 1s share was eventually worth 2s 6d.

- The NFWI mounted an exhibition at Caxton Hall, London to which Cornish institutes sent up pasties, saffron cakes, cheeses, needlework and other products.

- social concern has always been a central plank of the WI movement; in July 1918 Madron WI wrote to Madron Urban District Council (MUDC) regarding the 'lack of suitable sanitary accommodation in many of the houses'. A study circle learned about housing and town planning and one of their members stood for MUDC elections

- buying co-ops: for honey and fish

- charitable support: street collections for servicemen and for St Dunstan's were held.[137]

This is a very impressive first year for any organisation and was the pattern they were to follow. In fact Madron WI's first banner was made and embroidered in art nouveau script with the motto: 'Do all the good you can, in every way you can, to all the people you can.'

The pull-out map at the beginning of this book illustrates how scattered the farms and hamlets were. Without access to a car or bus some housewives were really isolated and 'never went anywhere' until the WI started encouraging and enabling them to become part of the village community. Although Madron was on a bus route by 1929, for many years members still mostly walked in groups from the outlying farms, hamlets and villages to the evening meetings.[138]

But if you couldn't get to the monthly meetings you could still stay in touch by reading the national Home and Country magazine, of which its founder said: 'Village will be united with village and county to county in a way that has never been possible before.'[139] Similarly, the County Newsletter (sometimes titled *The Cornishwoman*) gave news of local institutes, including a snapshot of Madron's activities; in the years 1920 and 1921, for example, there was a demonstration on 'Re-feeting stockings', a class on soldering, and a certificate of merit for Madron WI for 'rabbit wool gloves'. Miss Trant was the County Domestic Science Instructress and spent one week of her county-wide tour in Madron where she gave classes in 'dainty and appetising cookery…pretty supper dishes and other things, all of which were pronounced A1 by all. Her recipes of home-made metal polish and furniture polishes and distemper were in great demand, and the lesson in dry-starching and the use of the polishing iron, much appreciated.'[140]

Early in that decade Madron WI revived May Day celebrations, known as May Revels, in the village and organised an ambitious programme involving all the schoolchildren and probably every other inhabitant too; the events included a wagon decked with evergreens to carry the May Queen to Landithy Hall in a procession, the release of a basket of pigeons, maypole dancing, a 'bumper tea in the Hall', an evening concert with prizes, and a dance until midnight. May Day is celebrated in a similar fashion even today.[141] Just before the outbreak of World War II, the Cornwall Federation of

---

[136] Some recipes for home cures may have left the sufferer worse off, e.g. 'For baldness: Rub the part morning and evening with onions until red, and afterwards with honey'. Interestingly at the meeting I attended in January 2006, the 'bite to eat' included all the traditional sausage rolls, rock buns, mince pies and jam and cream sponge cakes which you would have found in 1918. In the 1920s, children's school lunch-boxes could contain a pasty (usually date and apple, but could be rabbit), aggie pudden, or figgie oggie. Madron WI:98
[137] Madron WI Minute Books.
[138] CPRE map; Madron WI meeting.
[139] NFWI *Fact Pack* (1944). *Home and Country* was started in 1919.
[140] *The Cornishwoman*, 1920-1. The Cornishwoman cost 2d in 1920
[141] Madron WI: 84-6; Madron WI meeting.

Women's Institutes (CFWI) County Rally was held at Trengwainton as guests of the Bolitho family, where 'over 900 teas were served. Helpers were from Madron, Newlyn West and Gulval WIs.'[142]

Referring back to my title *A Woman's Place?* you can see how the women of Madron village were encouraged and helped by their WI not only to develop their home-making skills but also to organise themselves into committees with a President, a Vice President, Secretary and Treasurer; they became speakers, demonstrators and voluntary county organisers; they spoke up at meetings and they were stimulated into an interest in the wider world. Members could also be involved on a county level once the CFWI was set up, and in fact Miss Bird, Mrs D. Le Grice and Mrs Bolitho all from Madron were early members of the executive committee of which Mrs D. Le Grice later became county president.[143] The regular debates focussed women's interest outside the family; some of the resolutions put forward by Cornish institutes before the last war still are being discussed today: the disposal of sewage (1920), reforms to practices in slaughterhouses (1921), 'the unwholesome influence of the cinema' (1923), the preservation of footpaths and commons (1926), the need for 'sufficient and sightly homes at low rentals in rural districts'(1938), and training women police officers to take statements from girls prior to court proceedings (1935).[144]

The May Queen and her attendants; the girls wore garlands while the boys had caps with pompoms. Undated but likely to be the early 1920s before the embroidered May Queen's cloak was made (Mary Laity's private collection)

One member who benefited from Madron WI at this time was Mrs A.: 'Granny said, 'You can't think of the difference in Mrs A. When she first came here she was so rough we couldn't do a thing with her, but she's been in the WI now long enough to realise what the WI really means in the village, and she's a completely changed person, because she's extremely intelligent.'[145]

---

[142] Donnelly: 11.

[143] *The Cornishwoman*, 1920-1

[144] Donnelly: 36; NFWI (1999): 1; NFWI, Coalville (1994): 46, 85. This reaction to the cinema was even before the introduction of the talkies in Penzance which happened in 1929. Perhaps members had in mind girls like those in Harold Harvey's bold painting of 'The Gaiety Girls' queuing outside the cinema in Newlyn (1925). Saundry's Almanac.

[145] Le Grice tape.

Although WI meetings have been normally held in the evenings after the main household chores are done, there was still some opposition in the early years from husbands who did not want their wives gallivanting about: '(It was) amazing (that they were allowed to join the WI)—well there were all sorts of nice cakes and things, and with any luck you might have won a pig so I suppose the men wouldn't have minded too much'.[146] The very real contribution women were making to the family budget during the Depression years would have helped to make the WI accepted by their menfolk; for example, the co-operative buying schemes were appreciated because, as their wives noted, 'the co-operative idea is a means of making the Institute of real practical value to individual members.'[147]

Mixing the Christmas pudding, 1934.
A typical family scene showing a Penzance interior (Morrab Library collection)

Wartime

By 1939 the NWFI was well established with 331,000 members in over 5,000 institutes in England and Wales, offering members the chance to participate in county rallies, produce markets, music and drama and above all to learn a surprising range of useful skills to a high standard.[148] During World War II WIs were particularly busy with their famous jam-making as well as with other schemes of salvaging waste paper, scrap metal, rags and bones; they also helped in the collection of plants for drugs (e.g. deadly nightshade, foxgloves, nettles, dandelion roots, broom, burdock, elder, rosehips and herbs), the rearing of rabbits and pigs for meat, and in collecting moleskins and live frogs.[149] The Fruit Preservation Scheme produced 36 tons (80,640 lbs) of jam from waste fruit in Cornwall alone, though it was noted that some institutes were more diligent than others; Madron WI filled 'only' 800 jars![150]

'Make do and Mend' was the catchphrase as all shop-bought articles were rationed. WIs were encouraged to set up children's shoe- and clothing-exchanges to save clothing coupons; alternatively

---

[146] Le Grice tape.
[147] *The Cornishwoman.*
[148] Goodenough: 47, 78-9; Jenkins: 16
[149] Ince: 80
[150] Donnelly: 27

clothes could be made from worn adult garments or you could 'combine two worn garments to make something fresh, and bring old-fashioned clothes up to date.' War meant privation, and invention.[151]

The WI movement was asked to take part in nationwide surveys by the government on the subjects of housing, water-supply and organisation of sewage, and education, showing the level of respect accorded to the organization. The Cornish response to the housing questionnaire placed an adequate water-supply as the first priority, followed by the need for women to be architects and housing committee members; one request was for 'room to bath baby between bed and fire'. The water and sewage survey found some extremely poor conditions, such as in Pendeen where '400 out of the 500 houses share pumps' and some households still had to pay for water delivered by cart; night soil was emptied once a week or fortnight by the council, or into the stream, ditch or garden. The education survey asked for better school buildings, lessons in citizenship, youth organisations, school funding to be national not local, and, revealingly, for 'textbooks with an international outlook'.[152]

Wartime also meant the arrival of thirty-nine evacuees in the village. Madron WI was at the heart of organising the children and their hosts. Host families were paid on a sliding scale from 8s6d to 15s per week, depending on the child's age, a useful addition to the family purse when an adult agricultural worker's wage was £1.14.6 (£1.72) a week.[153] 'Some of the 'vacuees were really nice kids,' said a local lady, who described one boy being given 'a boiled egg next day for breakfast, and bread and butter. And he didn't know what to do with it—never seen a boiled egg before!'[154] Mrs Le Grice spoke of some unexpected difficulties her upper middle-class family encountered:

Masses of children were put onto trains and sent down and we had six at Trereife; most successful, most successful. There was a funny little story: there were two boys aged about twelve and ten and Granny, my mother-in-law, used to make them change into clean white shirts every evening and wait at table; and I said to her 'You know Granny, you can't do this! These are not poor children sent to be nurtured, I mean they are our guests in the house.' 'I don't care' she said, 'we do a great deal for them and they can do a certain amount for us.' So they made the fire in the dining room and then waited at table. And then after the war, I was having lunch at The Liverpool Street Hotel and a very nice young man came up and said 'You don't know who I am, do you? Well I was Jimmy, your eldest evacuee. And I've never ceased to be thankful for your mother-in-law telling us how to wait at table. Look what it's done for me: I'm head waiter here!'[155]

WI members were able to respond to the improvement in local job-opportunities brought about by changing conditions; they were needed at Madron Isolation Hospital and on the Land Army farms at Trengwainton and Keneggy. Not surprisingly, the WI movement had been involved with the organisation of the Women's Land Army since 1938 when Lady Denman, chairman of the NFWI, was invited to become director of this scheme which trained women in farming skills and posted them to work on farms.

The post-war years

Women were less isolated after the war. Thanks to the increased expectations and opportunities brought about by the 1944 Education Act, the new National Health Service, improved transport and not least their own experiences during the war, women were now more actively integrated into the community (which had changed too of course). One example of how the WI movement helped women develop their potential capabilities is shown by Mary P., remembered here by Mrs Le Grice:

Mary went to church school for a little while then her mother wanted her to work and so she was taken away from school. But she was absolutely hot on the WI, and there was a resolution about pillar boxes, and Mary (she used to weigh nearly twenty stone, and absolutely fierce) went to the NFWI Annual General Meeting, in 1945 I think, and spoke to an Albert Hall full of women on her point. She was terrible though really! I was once made president again and I was rather pleased with myself; but as I came down off the stage in the evening, Mary P. came up to

---

[151] HMSO (1946).
[152] NFWI Water & Sewerage 1944; NFWI 1942; NFWI 1943.
[153] Ince: 16
[154] Starnes tape 2.
[155] Le Grice tape.

me and said 'Mrs Le Grice, doan 'ee ever wear that dress again! I doan like un, doesn't do a thing for 'ee.' And this was said with a room full of people listening![156]

And other members remember this formidable lady too:

Mary P. went up to the Albert Hall and spoke! A farmer's daughter, left school at 14 and went to work on the farm which belonged to the Le Grices. And later on she had a guest-house of her own, and then she went up as cook to Colonel Williams at Caerhays Castle. The WI gave you a lot of confidence for doing things, no doubt about it.[157]

Celebration dinner in Landithy Hall 1950 (Morrab Library collection)

After the hardships of the war years there was more time for fun, which was reflected in Madron WI's programme for 1948. This devoted greater time to entertainment and enjoyment, offering drama, parties, concerts, the May Revels, and outings as well as demonstrations and classes. 1948 was in fact a special year: the NFWI opened their very own Denman College (visited by a delegation from Madron WI) and the BBC, assuming a national audience, broadcast their AGM. Although some women still spent their working lives within the confines of the village, the job situation was gradually opening up: the Situations Vacant section of the *Cornishman* in 1958 had jobs for a State Registered Nurse, a sales lady, a book-keeper, a barmaid and a lady typist as well as three domestic vacancies.[158]

While items in the local paper still show signs of wartime stringency in 1948, by December 1958 the consumer revolution was in full swing. There were advertisements offering readers an astonishing range of equipment. Despite the fact that the average housewife was estimated to work 75 hours a week, '(m)ost of our people', said Prime Minister Harold Macmillan, 'have never had it so good'.[159]

Well, this was certainly true if you were able to take advantage of the easier credit available, for shops in Penzance tempted buyers with electrical vacuum cleaners, washing machines (with mangle), spin-dryers, clocks, blankets, kettles, irons, hair dryers, cookers, fridges, tea-makers, percolators, food mixers and toasters; in fact household appliances had become covetable items, something a woman

---

[156] Le Grice tape.
[157] Madron WI meeting.
[158] Starnes tape 2; *Cornishman* 2 Jan 1958.
[159] Carey: 53 citing an independent report; *The Times*, 22 July 1957, quoted in the *Guardian* of 26 Oct 2006.

would be pleased to receive as a Christmas present.[160] Certainly the growing availability of labour-saving appliances relieved women of hours of repetitive drudgery. Madron kept up with these innovations by inviting a South West Electricity Board cookery expert to give a demonstration, while the CWFI supported the new Consumer Research Council.[161] The extent of Madron WI's activities can be seen from the names of its sub-committees: entertainment, refreshments, handicrafts, competitions, flowers, votes of thanks, and bring & buy; the more serious business of talks, classes, demonstrations and produce markets must have been the responsibility of the whole committee.[162] And while the County Newsletters for 1958 report on the gardening classes, the produce guild and the drama festival we might associate with the WI, they also add some perhaps surprising items too: music conducting, a brains trust, a conference in Edinburgh for the Associated Countrywomen of the World, a course on modern painting, and one to mark the 1959 World Refugees Year on Families Without Homes. You could have participated in all those activities right here in Cornwall.

A Woman's Place?

What did Madron WI contribute to the life of the village? Did the Institute merely return members to their homes better skilled at preparing food and managing the family's welfare? Well, as far back as October 1920, Madron WI's entry in *The Cornishwoman* summed up their awareness of their power as a force for good: 'if the ordinary people in a village see a concrete example of what co-operation can do as against the efforts of any individual, it will do the Women's Institute a great good by giving it a name for practical results.' It is clear that the WI was an enriching experience which enlarged women's perspectives, encouraged their aspirations and nurtured their skills both at home and in the wider world. In Madron the institute inaugurated the week-long May Day Revels, helped set up the Madron Players, started buying co-operatives and savings schemes, held regular activities with other clubs, drew attention to social injustice, and supported local charities. The whole village has benefited by having confident and able women who are active in the community and who support one another.

As one long-term member reflected:

The WI gave you a lot of confidence for doing things, no doubt about it. We even had a confidence course! I tell you another thing, in this room is a lot of ladies that have had really sad lives. And I look at them and I think, how brave: there's S. her husband died of cancer, she was left with two children; and there's J. whose husband walked out and left her with three children, and so on. It's a thing where you got the support of other people; they support you. If you're left a widow you can come, even if you're feeling awkward. When things go wrong, we turn out to help, even now.[163]

But reflections mostly turned to the fun they have had in one another's company:

I really think that the WI from a woman's point of view, it was a real social occasion; I think it was probably more social than learning. Even during the second world war they used to have quite a lot of social evenings. [WI meetings were] fun, but the whole of the WI was fun really; I mean I did really get a tremendous lot out of it...taking it by and large it was a lively and very well organised group altogether.[164]

Conversely, a glance at the membership numbers is sadly revealing: the CFWI had 12 institutes in 1919, 239 by 1965 and 175 today (2006); Madron WI had 102 members in 1918, 88 in 1977 and 36 in 2006.[165] However, Madron WI is still flourishing because everyone agrees that it knows how to offer the right programme for its members, which is as it always was, a mixture of good cooking; interesting talks, classes and discussions; games; parties; entertainment, and above all, companionship.

---

[160] *Cornishman*, January and December 1948, 1958. Hire purchase restrictions were lifted on 29 October 1958 in time for Christmas.
[161] Madron WI Minutes 14 Oct 1958; *County Newsletter*, April 1958.
[162] Madron WI Minutes 25 Nov 1958.
[163] WI meeting.
[164] Le Grice tape.
[165] *Home & Country,* May 1965: 177; Iris Rowe 13 Nov 1906.

A full hall for the 40th anniversary celebration (1958).
The 1916 generation, like the WI in maturity.
(Mary Laity's private collection)

10. The Rise and Fall of a Penzance Business 1900-1959

Iris Green

The prime commercial site at the top of Market Jew Street known as numbers 5-9 Market Place, Penzance and extending westwards from the present Holland & Barrett (in 2006) to and including Wetherspoons, has seen much redevelopment over the course of time. The *Cornishman* newspaper of 4 May 1961 shows a large demolition site here: within just over a year it was to become Pearl Assurance House.[166] This particular development replaced what had been a thriving grocery, bakery and restaurant business, the expansion and subsequent decline of which had taken place during the first half of the twentieth century.

Price-lists of goods stocked, details of general management and minutes of the Board of Directors' meetings have been deposited at the Morrab Library, Penzance by Jeffrey Turner, great-grandson of the founder of a business established in 1857.[167] Supplemented by local newspaper reports and researched by David Chinn, to whom I am most grateful, this archive provides an insight into ways in which a business developed and then declined to the point of closure in a period of great and rapid social change at the beginning of the last century. The announcement of the closing of R Chirgwin & Son Ltd, to take effect from the end of September 1959, was made in the *Cornishman* on 20 August that year:

> *This marked the passing of one of the old West of England family grocery firms which had been a landmark in Penzance and district for over a hundred years. The decision to close affects all branches of their activities—groceries and provisions in the main shop, the bakery and confectionery departments, the restaurant and the café; the premises in the Market Place are being taken over by new owners for complete reconstruction.[168]*

Branches established at St Mary's (Isles of Scilly), Newlyn, St Ives, St Just and Heamoor had already been closed.

The Newlyn branch, said to be a 'very fine shop,' was constructed on the site of Thomas Marrack's house in Street-an-Nowan where a Chinese café now stands. It had been bought in 1895 by Percy Teague Chirgwin, son of the founder of the business, for £330.[169] The St Just branch was at 18 Bank Square where the News Centre now stands. Because of local competition Chirgwin's here was soon taken over by first the International Stores, then Peark's, Lipton's and Presto's in turn. Finally, four days after Christmas 1988, because it was still losing money, it became a newsagent, book and stationery store.[170] Chirgwin's on the Isles of Scilly remained their only grocery store for fifty years. I am told that the name is still preserved over another shop in St Mary's.

Richard Chirgwin began this business at 7 Market Place in 1857, advertising it with a handwritten notice to his friends in Penzance and thereabouts. When he died in 1879 at the age of forty-six, his widow (who survived him by twenty-six years) continued until such time as their only son Percy Teague Chirgwin took control. In 1905, the year in which his mother died, Percy was the National President of the Grocers' Federation, and the Annual Conference was held in Penzance. He was a man of ambition who, in partnership with his brother-in-law Fred Jarvis, built up the business by opening new branches as already mentioned and, at their main establishment in Penzance, by adding to the grocery store a bakery, and entering into the catering trade.

The advertisement on the next page appeared in Kelly's 1902 Trade Directory. It shows that the already established grocery business needed no further promotion apart from a few items. At this time, soup produced by Lazenby's was sold in squares, not packets or tins, jellies were 3/6d per quart, cream was 4/6d a quart[171]—delicacies for the well-to-do of the neighbourhood, together with fresh cream and butter from Chirgwins' own farm only a mile from town. This was probably in the water-meadows

---

[166] *Cornishman* 4 May 1961:12, and 15 November 1962:11. For full bibliographical information, see the Bibliography on pp. 113-116
[167] Chirgwin Archive.
[168] *Cornishman* 20 August 1959:5.
[169] *Cornish Telegraph* 4 July 1895:8.
[170] Hughes.
[171] All prices quoted in this article are in pre-decimalisation terms.

from the Minney or Mennaye towards Newlyn Coombe. This was where Percy Teague had been born, though he was later recorded as living at Chywoone Farm, to the west of Newlyn.

MACHINE BAKERY.

R. CHIRGWIN & SON,

BAKERS AND CONFECTIONERS,

7 & 8, Market Place, PENZANCE.

→ LUNCHEON ✦ ROOMS. ←

Artistic Bride Cakes always in Stock, and Special Designs made to order.

. . . . Soups, Creams, Jellies, Ices, Gingerbreads, Macaroons, &c. . . . .

Fresh CREAM and BUTTER Daily from Home Farm.

This was not the grocer for the labouring classes. Farming folk produced their own cream and butter and sold to their neighbours, grew their own vegetables, kept chickens, baked their own bread, caught rabbits and perhaps had a stew-pot permanently simmering to provide a nourishing soup. In semi-urban areas of small cottages, use was made of communal bake houses.

The most innovative of Chirgwin's developments, and one promoted in this advertisement, was the establishment of a machine bakery. Machinery had been supplied by J Baker & Son of London and used to produce a wide range of bread and confectionery (e.g. cakes). Household bread was made in different shapes and weights—kettles, uprights, squares, cottages, crusties, as well as wholemeal and patent germ bread ranging in price from 1d to 6d. Fancy bread included 1/4d tough cakes, Vienna rounds and sandwich rolls, as well as 2d milk cottage loaves. These were being produced 1892-93 and all orders were delivered, firstly to shops in rural communities and then to individual households as more and more women became involved in work on the farm, and had less time for home cooking.

Chirgwin's confectionery department used the bakery to produce a large variety of cakes and buns— saffron, rice, coconut, sultana, Genoa, nine varieties of rich cakes and ten of small cakes. Bride cakes at 1/8d a pound were always kept in stock ready to be ornamented. They baked thirty varieties of tarts, some sweet and some savoury. Not all were available for daily sale in their main shop but orders placed the day before were then delivered the following day.

This firm was famed for baking powder of its own manufacture, as shown in an 1895 testimonial from Adeline M Evans, Principal of the Penzance School of Technical Education for Women and Girls. She wrote: 'During the period I have been connected with the Penzance School of Cookery I have used your Baking Powder at all my classes. I have never known it to fail and consider it one of the best I have ever tried.' Praise indeed for such a humble product!

Chirgwin's had always been keen to advertise their tea and coffee, and to ensure that these beverages were correctly brewed. Price-lists of 1909 and 1913 gave these instructions:

A hot dry Earthenware Jug

A generous measure (one ounce for each pint) of Chirgwin's Pure Coffee

Infuse with boiling water; stir thoroughly.

Let it stand five minutes. Serve with cream.

Result: PERFECTION

Coffee prices ranged from 1/0d to 1/10d per pound. Much was made of their celebrated teas at 1/4d to 2/10d a pound. They are blended to suit the water of the district, their special blend of pure china tea at 2s per pound being recommended by the medical profession. As far as is known, the only shop in Penzance still selling pure ground coffee and loose tea is Lavender's delicatessen in Alverton Street.

Booklets of Christmas specialities of 1909 and 1913 show the very wide range of products stocked in this grocery and provision business.Dried fruits (cleaned by the most up-to-date machinery), crystallised and glace fruits, preserved ginger, tinned and bottled fruits. Tins of pineapple chunks cost 1/6d, 2s and 3s, cheddar, Stilton, Gorgonzola, Roquefort, Gruyere, Parmesan and cream cheeses are listed without prices. Cooked pressed beef, tongues, over twenty cuts of ham, Palethorpe's celebrated sausages (as supplied to all the great Atlantic liners), seven varieties of nuts and a large selection of fresh green fruit in season.

A one-pound jar of mincemeat cost 10d, plum puddings in china moulds were 1s per pound. Moulds were free. Huntley & Palmer fancy biscuits were in ornamental tins and cost 6d to 3/6d each. Tom Smith's Christmas crackers at 6d to 6s per box and Fuller's and Carson's chocolates and sweets were also stocked, so were continental specialities such as liver sausage, salami de Milano, sauerkraut, burnt onions and Bombay ducks at 7½d a tin. Tins of Heinz baked beans in tomato sauce and soups appear on the shelf. All kinds of poultry trussed ready for the table were sold.

A hundred years ago grocery, bakery and hardware shops were quite often combined. Chirgwin's was no exception. Besides their bakery, this store sold over a hundred items of patent medicines, hardware and all manner of brushes. There were brushes to clean banisters, grates, clothes, carpets, horses, shoes and pictures. The price-list contained drawings of each. This wide variety of high-quality products shows that Chirgwin's catered mainly for the more affluent of the population of West Penwith—a niche market that could, and did, change.

An article from the *Grocer and Oil Trade Review*, reported in the *Evening Tidings*, is worth quoting at length for the insight it gives into Percy Chirgwin's success:

...a success achieved by personal ability, keenness of perception, with perhaps a spice of judicious speculation. On leaving Queen's College, Taunton in 1882, Mr Chirgwin, though only seventeen years old, immediately entered the business established by his father and which was the oldest grocery business in the town——With the exuberance and ambition of youth, Mr Chirgwin set his heart on enlarging and expanding the scope of operations. After four years, he rebuilt the premises, took in additional ground and started a bakery and confectionery business. Since that time, the premises have been once more enlarged until now one of the largest retail trades is done from the Market Place establishments.

Percy J. Chirgwin

President of the Federation of Grocers' Associations, 1905, and President of the Penzance and District Grocers and Provision Dealers' Association.

Though the demands of the trade have been heavy, Percy Chirgwin has found time to interest himself in a number of town movements, and to take an active part in the social and municipal life of the borough. For three years he was a member of the Corporation, but he did not find the work very palatable and on the expiration of his term of office did not seek re-election——He is chairman of the Penzance Gas Company, Football and cricket clubs he has enthusiastically supported and Freemasonry has given him various rewards for diligent service——The value of trade organisations naturally impressed itself upon him, and he was the prime mover in the formation of the Penzance Grocers' Association. On several occasions he has filled various offices within this Association. He has also presided over the Council of the West Cornwall Grocers' Associations which comprises the important towns of Truro, Redruth, Camborne and Penzance——The resuscitation of the Penzance Chamber of Commerce, which a few years ago had a lamentable death from neglect, is in large measure due to Mr Chirgwin and it is now a real live, useful local institution, which promises to accomplish much valuable work in the development of the resources of the town. His hobbies are pedigree Guernsey cattle and flowers—each of which brings him untold wealth in prizes at local shows.

Mr Chirgwin is looking forward with much pleasure, mingled with some amount of trepidation, to the visit to Penzance next July of the Federation. It is a great undertaking for a borough of thirteen thousand inhabitants; but the Cornish are a hospitable, generous race, the county is full of natural grandeur, grace and beauty and it will not be from lack of effort or of good feeling if the Penzance conference is not to be included amongst the most pleasurable and successful in the list.'[172]

Richard Chirgwin Jun (Courtesy of Morrab Library)

Percy Chirgwin died in January 1918 in an accident on a ferry journey to the Scillies and his partner Fred Jarvis died in 1926. Their sons Richard Chirgwin Jun and Richard Cyril Jarvis were appointed joint Managing Directors under Mrs Chirgwin, widow of Percy Teague, and later also Mrs Jarvis, widow of Fred Jarvis. This partnership introduced further new developments and might have continued successfully but for the untimely death in 1930 of Richard Chirgwin Jun from pneumonia at the age of twenty-nine.

Richard Chirgwin was born on 15 February 1901 at the Minney or Mennaye Estate, Penzance, the third child and only son of Percy Teague and Agatha (formerly Polglase). He was educated at Wycliffe College, Stonehouse, Gloucestershire, from 1912-18. He remained a bachelor and lived at Trevellyn, Alexandra Road.

He was responsible for rebuilding, refurbishment and refronting at the Market Place premises. The bow windows of the luncheon-rooms above the grocer's shop were replaced by bay windows and sashes so common in Penzance today. Its interior was turned into a 'luxurious' restaurant with separate marble-topped tables with waitresses in black and white uniforms reminiscent of Lyons Corner House in London.

---

[172] *Evening Tidings,* 11 May 1905 (cost ½d).

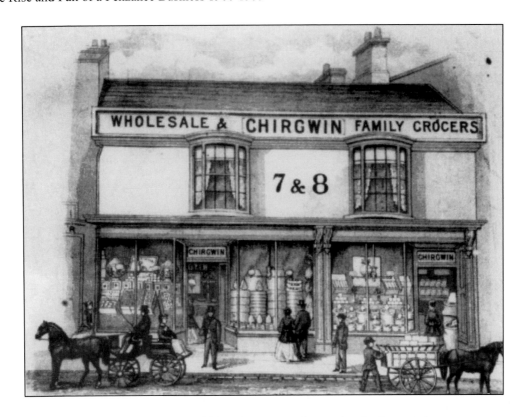

The early shop with luncheon room above, showing bow windows.
(Courtesy of Morrab Library, Penzance)

The modernised shop and restaurant with bays and sash window
(Courtesy of Morrab Library, Penzance)

Some idea of the dynamic personality of Richard Chirgwin Jun can be gained from Penzance's reaction to his early death. In his short life, besides being joint-manager of Chirgwin & Co. he was member of the Master Bakers' and Master Grocers' Federation, chairman of the Chamber of Commerce, a Rotarian and member of the committee of West Cornwall Hospital as well as business manager and then general manager of the Penzance Amateur Operatic Society. It was here that he met Crosbie Garstin, an artist, who with his wife, were active members of the group.

Garstin wrote a tribute to 'beloved Dick' and Mrs WET Bolitho, President of the *Cornish Evening Tidings*, wrote: 'he was one of those, of whom I might say "he lit fires in cold rooms"'. On the day of his funeral all Penzance businesses closed. His early death may well have contributed to the firm's decline from 1930 onwards.

Descendants of Richard Chirgwin

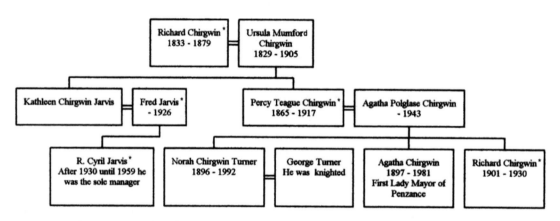

*The first managers of the main business

The legacy that Richard Chirgwin Jun left was certainly the restaurant. In the early days of the Chirgwin restaurant prices were said to be moderate. A plate of ham, tongue or beef cost 6d. Tea, coffee or cocoa was 3d a cup. Parnall, store fitters of Bristol, supplied shop-fittings for the modernisation of the grocery and provision shop.

Many Penzance residents of today remember with pleasure their special treats at this smart meeting place. For many years this restaurant that had been modernised in 1928 was the only establishment of its kind in the town. It provided excellent accommodation for wedding receptions and evening parties. Young Farmers' Clubs met here at times. (Later in the century, the Queen's Hotel on the Promenade took over the function of hosting large-scale events.)

With several rural branches in addition to its main store, there was a need for capital and careful, efficient management. Was expansion too fast or were there factors outside the firm's control that led to falling profits? In 1919, after Percy Chirgwin's death, the business was registered as a private limited company with £1 shares. Dividends and bonuses were paid to shareholders and to members of the Board of Directors from the firm's profits. It is from minutes of their meetings that the gradual decline in profitability from the 1930s onwards can be traced. For example, in the Penzance shop in 1931 it was recorded that thirty fewer bags of flour had been ordered in the bakery but that turnover was £1600 less: prices had fallen rather than trade been lost. A study of prices made by the St Just WI for the period 1905-2000[173] shows that after the boom years of the 1920s, the price of many foods had fallen close to the 1914 level. Butter, sugar, flour, potatoes, eggs and bread all showed this trend. Falling prices reflected the national situation in 1932 when nearly three million—one in four of the British labour force—were unemployed. Official statistics excluded many agricultural workers, the

---

[173] This price list is reproduced with the pull-out map at the beginning of the book.

self-employed and married women. Agriculture was one of the main occupations in Cornwall and although the labouring classes were not Chirgwin's main clientele there must have been some declining trade due to the national depression[174]. There were fewer visitors reported in August and September from 1937-9 though on the 16 July 1959, two months before closure, 'a nice drop of drizzle sent visitors in for shelter'. Today Penzance traders are still none too pleased with 'beach weather'.

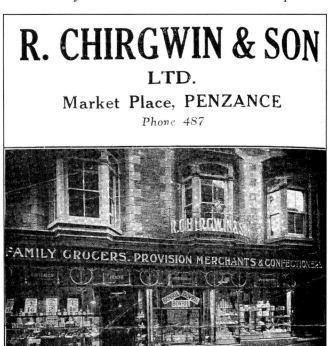

Competition from the multiple store was the major threat to trade in Chirgwin's Penzance grocery business. The age of out-of-town supermarkets came at the end of the century, but in his report to the Board of Directors in the mid 1930s, Cyril Jarvis, nephew of P T Chirgwin and managing director of the firm, mentioned the Co-operative Society Ltd. Competition was also felt in St Just where Chirgwin's had a branch in 1935. It was not long before it was taken over by the International Stores. Many smaller grocery outlets became mini-markets when packaging replaced the selling loose of commodities such as sugar, tea, dried fruits and biscuits, weighed and bagged for each customer. Butter and cooking salt were no longer cut from a large block.

Fortunes at the Newlyn branch ebbed and flowed depending on trade with boats and on Admiralty contracts. Although the fishing families did not usually shop here, even the better-off deserted for the wider choice in Penzance. Despite a reduction in staff, continuing trading losses resulted in closure in 1957, making it possible to negotiate a £9,000 overdraft which kept the firm going in its final two years.

---

[174] Heald, 1081.

The branch on the Isles of Scilly was most successful. Between 1929 and 1931 it showed the greatest turnover, but even here trade had fallen by 1936. Beetles had caused some losses but fiddling at the till needed to be watched. Absence of competition enabled this store to survive for fifty years.

In addition to competition, rapid improvements in mobility altered patterns of shopping and also the running costs of a business expanding into rural areas. The replacement of horse-drawn vehicles by motor-vans for deliveries required capital outlay. In St Ives in 1930, an Austin 7 was bought for Mr Gray who collected orders, but the purchase of a Ford 8 to replace the horse vehicle for deliveries was delayed when the Golf Club business was lost. In the early years of the twentieth century most people walked to Penzance from the various centres of population within West Penwith. From 1890 to 1920 the Royal Mail coach provided four regular services six days a week with an extra one on market days from St Just to Penzance. Motor-buses followed. The pony and trap for personal mobility was superseded by the motor-car. Land behind the Star Inn, Market Jew Street, provided early parking facilities for horses and traps, as did the lower part of the street itself. Choice of where to shop was ever widening.

Nevertheless, not everything could be blamed on the national situation or on social developments beyond the firm's control. A lack of good management, particularly in the branches, was evident. When the St Ives branch showed a deficit of £100 a visit by the managing director showed the cellar door open and no one in attendance! The manager was ordered to put on a lock. He was made responsible for the wine stock as well as grocery and provisions—a pretty obvious action of good management. By 1939 the St Ives branch had closed.

Bad debts were a concern and in 1940 a list of major debtors was drawn up. They were in Lamorna, Porthcurno, Porthleven, St Just, Mousehole, Scilly, Marazion and Heamoor, and the onus for recovery was placed on branch managers. Since these debts amounted to over £1,000, they were evidently not doing their job. It was admitted, too, that staff in all the branches needed a good talking-to.

Mrs Jarvis, a family member, regarded the firm's collapse as a 'distressing failure' but in its hundred years' history, there were periods of considerable success in an era of rapid change. In the latter part of the twentieth century, this change in retailing has continued. Out-of-town supermarkets are expanding from grocery into the provision of other goods and services. Besides hardware and eating places, clothing, petrol, banking, insurance, holidays and dry-cleaning are all catered for in one establishment. Will internet shopping lead to a further re-organisation of the retail trade?

Father, son and grandson of the Chirgwin family established their successful business in a town which a century ago had developed a new commercial identity. In 1905, an article in the *Evening Tidings* began:

> *Penzance is the Mecca of the tourist in Cornwall. The westernmost town in England, it is a charmingly situated borough nestling in the bight of a magnificent bay, an ideal resting place for the jaded city toiler.*
>
> *A few years ago it seemed as though the commercial glories of Penzance had vanished with the closing of the rich tin and copper mines which stretched east and west for miles, but from the ashes of a grimy and unlovely mining industry there has been evolved a far more fitting occupation for the residents of a picturesque and beautifully endowed land—the reception and entertainment of health seekers and holiday makers.*[175]

If we could look ahead another century, would we see Penzance retain this identity or would there be another, due perhaps to poor husbanding of resources or competition from abroad? Could even the beauty of the bay be spoilt by an excessive development of sea sports and marinas, the landscape by new houses, new roads and car parks? Could the health-giving fresh air become polluted by fuel emissions?

How might the possible killing of the 'goose that laid the golden egg' be prevented or will some other source of commercial identity be achieved for Penzance and the Mount's Bay region? Just as over-speculation, weak organisation, development in mobility and competition led to the decline of a single business in the first half of the twentieth century, could a similar fate befall the tourist trade in Penzance by the end of the twenty first century? Few of us will ever know.

---

[175] *Evening Tidings*, 11 May 1905.

11. Wheal Betsy Cottage: An Arts & Crafts House in Newlyn

Pamela Lomax

'We have made of a great social movement a narrow, tiresome little aristocracy working with great skill for the very rich' (Charles Robert Ashbee, 1907)[176]

We drove past the Passmore Edwards Art Gallery, over the bridge into the fishing village of Newlyn then up the hill towards Paul. Chywoone Hill (pronounced 'Choone') has not changed much since Newlyn Bridge was built in 1884 and the modern topography of Newlyn was created. Property was demolished directly in front of the bridge to create Bucca's Pass, a short stretch of road to join Chywoone Hill at the junction with Jack Lane, which had been the main road from Newlyn to Paul.

Wheal Betsy Cottage (John Lewington & Company, House Details)

It was on Chywoone Hill that the artist Thomas Cooper Gotch and his wife Caroline Burland Yates built Wheal Betsy in 1910. Although almost invisible from the hill, Wheal Betsy is situated in a commanding position with a bird's eye view of the bustling and busy fishing port of Newlyn and panoramic views of St Michael's Mount and Mount's Bay. On that first visit in 1996 we turned sharp right near the top of the hill, past the garage and right again into the forecourt of the house. This small forecourt is dominated by the east-facing porch of the house which welcomes the rising sun as well as its visitors; in fact the grey granite house with slate-hung elevations and horizontal white-painted casement windows made of many panes of leaded glass stands squarely on the four compass points. The most dramatic feature of Wheal Betsy is its broad overhanging eaves and hipped random slate roof, broken by the two tall brick chimneystacks that run straight up and out half way down the slope of the roof. Originally they would have been covered in roughcast with lead cresting and dumpy louvered chimney pots fitted with a variety of cowls and deflectors to improve the draw.

---

[176] Yorke: 50. For full bibliographical details, see the Bibliography on pp. 113-116.

Wheal Betsy was built in the Arts and Crafts style of the early part of the short-lived international movement that started in England and is associated with the beginnings of Modernism and twentieth-century values.[177] Its wide influence included the design of domestic buildings and their interiors. In architecture it was a reaction to the ugliness of the industrial revolution and it sought to create beautiful houses through craftsmanship, traditional building methods and the use of natural materials. The movement emerged at the end of the nineteenth century in a number of different artistic circles, of which architecture was only one. It is important to remember that it was a social and artistic movement as well as a style. Thus one of its earliest advocates, John Ruskin, championed handcraft rather than machine-craft because it was made by ordinary men who were masters of their own work and not slaves to machinery. Another early advocate, William Morris, was a socialist who campaigned for better conditions for craftsmen. He thought that the workers' involvement in a process from beginning to end would prevent their alienation (a very Marxist idea). Morris commissioned the architect Philip Webb to build The Red House in 1859, and this became the 'emblematic start'[178] for the new style. Webb favoured a vernacular architecture based on old English farmhouses, which may explain why Thomas Cooper Gotch chose to call his new house Wheal Betsy *Cottage*.

The ideas of Ruskin and Morris provided the original principles upon which the Arts and Craft Movement was formed, and although these principles were to be associated with a number of different architectural styles that were to span about 100 years, there were important commonalities. Most Arts and Crafts architects followed Ruskin's lead in abandoning the formal, symmetrical elevations of late Renaissance architecture in favour of mediaeval lines with irregular plans. According to the architect Hermann Muthesius, writing in 1907, 'the essence of modern arts and crafts' was 'a firm grasp of each item's particular purpose' and as a logical consequence 'devising the appropriate form'. It rejected 'an emphasis on appearance leading to imitation and the use of substitute materials such as stamped pasteboard for wood, sheet zinc for stone and tin castings for bronze'.[179]

Arnold Mitchell, the architect of Wheal Betsy, was to favour the values and styles associated with the work of Webb's contemporary, Richard Norman Shaw, who was largely responsible for the 'very eclectic style so absurdly miscalled Queen Anne',[180] which favoured tile-hung facades, overhanging eaves, horizontal bands of small paned casement windows and prominent porches.[181] All these architectural features can be seen at Wheal Betsy.

But why was Wheal Betsy built as an Arts and Crafts house in Newlyn in the first decade of the new century?

The clients

It was not surprising that the Gotches chose to build their new house in Newlyn as they had personally witnessed the changing face of Newlyn since their first visit as young art students in 1879, before it was an artists' colony. In fact they married in Newlyn in 1881, and for thirteen years from 1887 they lived half way up Chywoone Hill in a house that was converted from an old Malt House. After six years in London, the Gotches returned to Newlyn in 1906. They had survived the economic depression with which the twentieth century had started and were feeling the benefits of the strengthening economy. Like many other modest, though prosperous professionals, they sought a smaller residence like those featured in the English periodical, *The Studio*, which was launched in 1893 to promote the new Arts and Crafts movement.

The Gotches were already familiar with Arts and Crafts principles when *The Studio* was launched.[182] As art students in London in 1878, Tom Gotch and Caroline Yates were interested onlookers at the famous libel trial when James McNeill Whistler was awarded a farthing damages against Ruskin who had accused him of charging two hundred guineas 'for flinging a pot of paint in the public's face'.[183] Ruskin's view of Whistler's art mirrored that 'peculiarly English rejection of

---

[177] Livingstone & Parry: 10-40.
[178] Dempsey: 19.
[179] Muthesius: 38.
[180] *The Studio* V No 25 April 1895: 67-74
[181] Calloway: 306.
[182] Lomax (a): 13-19.
[183] Anderson & Koval: 218.

modernity' which was to be associated with Arts and Crafts values. It was most strongly reflected in the 'obsession amongst the middle classes for a mythical rural past, handmade crafts, rustic cottages and country ways'.[184]

Caroline Gotch c.1900 (Private Collection), Thomas Cooper Gotch, 1908 (Private Collection)

The young Gotch's interest in Arts and Crafts is suggested in a letter he received from his friend Henry Paget who wrote, 'I've told a fellow named Campbell to call upon you in London… He's a great disciple of Ruskin's and I think you'll find him interesting. He is… going to regenerate Art through the working classes, in the Morris sort of way.'[185] Six years later, Gotch was in the front line of the debate about Arts and Crafts that led to its metamorphosis from a set of principles into a fully fledged movement.[186] It happened because of his involvement from 1886 in the formation of the very radical New English Art Club. Its members (mainly painters) opposed the elitism and commercialism of the Royal Academy. Their views were shared by young architects.

On the one hand was the Royal Academy, chartered for Architecture, Painting and Sculpture alike, but now giving its favour almost entirely to oil painting, allowing to architecture a membership of five out of a total of seventy… On the other hand there was the Royal Institute of British Architects, whose theory of architecture had driven from its doors most of those architects whose art was acknowledged; which had forbidden to Artists a personal interest in their handicrafts and had opened its doors so widely to business that Surveyors had become the largest body.[187]

Unfortunately, the first exhibition of the New English Art Club held on 12 April 1886 showed only paintings done in oil, which reflected the hierarchical view of the arts that the most radical of the new artists wanted to destroy. There was a move for a National Exhibition to cover all branches of the arts, including craft that would be run by the artists and be independent of the art establishment. Walter Crane, George Clausen and Holman Hunt took the lead and the provisional committee that was formed included the architects Richard Norman Shaw and Philip Webb, and the painters Thomas Cooper Gotch and Stanhope Forbes. Although a national exhibition was never organised, an Arts & Crafts Exhibition Society was formed with Walter Crane as the first president and in 1887 the name *Arts and Crafts Movement* was coined by one of the members, TJ Cobden-Sanderson.

---

[184] Yorke: 15.
[185] Tate Archive: HM Paget to TC Gotch, 19 March 1880.
[186] Lomax (b): 62-83.
[187] Gray: 44.

These early experiences were important, but a more significant influence on Tom Gotch was his brother, J Alfred Gotch, a distinguished architect[188] who was closely associated with many Arts and Crafts Architects, such as Gerald Horsley (who had worked with Norman Shaw), Edward Prioleau Warren (the architect of the Fishermen's Mission in Newlyn) and Edwin Lutyens (with whom J. A. Gotch later collaborated to build the Midland Bank's London Headquarters). All four men were members of the influential Foreign Architectural Book Society (FABS), a Society in which membership was limited to fifteen architects at any one time. Edwin Lutyens became a member in 1909, the same year J Alfred Gotch was responsible for the annual recreational meeting of the Society, organising visits to Kettering (Gotch's home town), Drayton and Kirby. The invited guests for this three-day meeting were Bertram McKennal and TC Gotch.[189] The conversation must have moved to the new house that TC Gotch was planning and it seems likely that the company recommended the architect Arnold Mitchell, who had worked with Lutyens.

Tom Gotch knew Arnold Mitchell well: he had previously done watercolour portraits of Mitchell's children Olive (1900), Edward (1901) and Rosamund (1905). At the time of the FABS recreational meeting, during June and July 1909, he was painting an oil portrait of Rosamund at the Mitchells' home Great Baddow near Chelmsford,[190] and it seems likely that Gotch approached Mitchell to design Wheal Betsy at that time. One can imagine the conversation being similar to one Gertrude Jekyll had with her architect Edwin Lutyens: 'I said that I wanted a small house with plenty of room in it – there are seven bedrooms in all - and that I disliked small narrow passages, and would have nothing poky or screwy or ill-lighted'.[191] Jekyll went on to describe how the architect drew the plan, and how they talked over every portion and had many an amicable fight; the same would have been the case for Gotch and Mitchell although I expect that Arnold Mitchell had a much easier time from the amiable Gotch than did Lutyens from Jekyll.

If Arnold Mitchell was commissioned to build Wheal Betsy in July 1909, it would have been one year after the building lease for Wheal Betsy was finalised between Gotch and the land owner, Thomas Leah, on 20 July 1908, and sometime before Gotch sent his plans to Paul Urban District Council on 3 November 1909 (PUDC Minutes, CRO DC Pen 286). It may be significant that (unusually) no price was recorded next to the record of Rosamund Mitchell's portrait in Gotch's MSS. Was the fee for the portrait waived in lieu of the fee for the architect's drawings for Wheal Betsy?

The architects

Arnold Bidlake Mitchell (1863-1944), though not one of the élite Arts and Crafts architects, was well respected and successful. He was articled to Robert Stark Wilkinson in 1880 and trained in Sir Ernest George's office. In 1884 he entered the Royal Academy Schools and won the Soane Medallion (1885) and the Silver Medal for Drawings (1886). He started in practice in 1887 and became a fellow of the RIBA in 1894. In the first decade of the twentieth century Mitchell was a darling of *Studio* magazine, and many of his large country houses were featured in it, including The Willows at Northwood, Barnett Hill near Guildford, Toys Hill at Brasted, and King Leopold of Belgium's Royal Villa at Le Coq-sur-Mer. He designed two houses in Paul Parish, Wheal Betsy and Trevelloe House. Trevelloe House was built in 1911 for WET Bolitho, and is the only listed Arts and Crafts house in the parish.

Perhaps one of the reasons that the Gotches chose Arnold Mitchell as their architect was that his strongest quality was said to be his ability to get the most out of unpromising sites.[192] In this he followed in the steps of his teacher, Ernest George, who wrote, 'A satisfactory building owes no little to its environment—certainly the problem to make it accord with its surroundings, harmoniously but not too arrogantly, is one of the most difficult that confronts the architect.'[193]

Wheal Betsy is built on the side of a north-facing hill just above a quarry. It was called Wheal Betsy because it was on the site of the short-lived Wheal Elizabeth mine, which was opened in 1851 and

---

[188] He was the first provincial President of RIBA, 1923-5.

[189] Newton: 29.

[190] Tate Archive: Tom Gotch to Caroline Gotch, 11 July 1909.

[191] Jekyll: 34.

[192] *The Architect and Building News,* 10 November 1944: 89

[193] *The Studio*, V??? No 39 June 1896: 27

went out of business in 1853[194]. On 9 January 1908 (the year the Gotches acquired the lease for the Wheal Betsy plot), the *Cornishman* reported that the main shaft at 'the old and locked knacked bal known as Wheal Betsy at Fawgan' had been capped with iron girders and covered with cement. Although this shaft was probably outside the Wheal Betsy plot, there was an older shaft to the south called Flat Rod Shaft that was re-opened in 1853 and was probably on the Wheal Betsy plot.[195] The Gotches must have been aware of the mine-workings close to the site of their new house, but no provision was made to deal with them in the original building specification, so the work came as an extra, costing £3-14s-4d, which provided for fifteen hours from a mason, fifty-two hours from a labourer and eighteen loads of stones.[196]

Mitchell was unaware of the 'old men' (the old mine workings), and his main challenge in designing Wheal Betsy was that the house was to be built on the side of the hill. True to the Arts and Crafts principle that new buildings should integrate with the surrounding landscape, Mitchell built the north-facing side three storeys high and the south-facing side two storeys high, so that the house nestles into the hillside. This was not a new design for Mitchell, being similar to his own house, Grove Hill Cottage in Harrow, the drawings for which were shown at the RA in 1893.

Wheal Betsy North East Corner (P Lomax)

Grove Hill Cottage[197] was built in 'a limited space on a site facing east and west, and falling thirty feet in two hundred feet with an even greater fall north to south'. Wheal Betsy Cottage lies on the 300-foot contour and there is a fall of ten feet in the south-to-north direction. The land slopes gently to the sea in the east but there is a steep drop to a valley in the west. Grove Hill had eleven rooms on nine different levels, while Wheal Betsy Cottage had fifteen rooms on eleven levels. 'However seriously the arrangement might be criticised in a mansion', wrote Mitchell, 'it is certainly apt and picturesque in the cottage.'[198] Because of the steep decline of the land at Grove Hill, Mitchell arranged the staircase (without stairwell) in the centre and planned the rooms to open off the many landings; there were no corridors. The arrangement at Wheal Betsy is similar; there is a turning staircase directly across the entrance hall from the front door, with a prominent landing from which Caroline Gotch could greet her visitors. From there another short flight of steps leads to a split landing with steps to both right and left leading to other landings from which the bathrooms and bedrooms fan out. When we first moved into the house we had difficulty getting our bearings and had to put number-plates on the upstairs rooms.

It was said that Arnold Mitchell believed that the architect's function was to identify for the client what he wanted and to get it for him, but he could not afford the time commitment that the 'wandering architects' gave to their work. These men were true to the letter of the Arts and Crafts ideal that architects should be involved in the full process of the work, including hands on building work. For example when Philip Tilden built the nearby Buckshead House at Townshend for Dr Vyvian in 1911, he lived near the site, participated in the building work until the house was completed, and signed his drawings, 'architect and builder'. 'Those were the years to build in', he wrote, 'that was the time when we could do what we liked with what we liked, to create those little eccentricities arising from exigencies which makes a design grow.'[199]

---

[194] Hamilton Jenkins : 16-17
[195] Hamilton Jenkin: 16-17.
[196] Wheal Betsy Archive: Builders Contract between T.C. Gotch and Ed. Pidwell, Builder and Contractor
[197] *The Studio,* XV No 67 October 1898: 168-74.
[198] *The Builders Journal and Architectural Record,* December 2 1896: 259.
[199] Drury: 199-214.

Although Wheal Betsy was inspired by the ideals of the early Arts and Crafts Movement, in many ways it was a compromise. The clients could not afford the original workmanship and finest materials that were features of the great Arts and Crafts houses and the architect could not afford to work on site. Mitchell made some visits, such as that mentioned by the builder Pidwell in a letter to Gotch: 'You remember when Mr Mitchell was down when we were putting the woodwork on for the roof, he asked me to put dragon pieces at each external angle of the main building;'[200] but Mitchell was at Hanover Square in London for most of the building period. Given the importance in Arts and Crafts architecture of local building materials and traditional building methods, it is not surprising that Gotch also employed the local architect and surveyor, Henry Maddern.

Henry Maddern came from an old Newlyn family. His mother, Elizabeth Maddern, ran a lodging house at 'Lesser' Belle Vue. Belle Vue was the focal point of the artist community in the 1880s with many of the artists staying there. The Gotches would have known the Maddern family. Stanhope Forbes described Mrs. Maddern as 'a nice old dame' in one letter, and in another letter in which he complains about the Gotches 'absurd way of dressing their sweet little girl,' Forbes confides, 'Mrs. Maddern is very shocked. "Oh Mr. Forbes, I do call it wrong".'[201]

Henry's father of the same name was described as a joiner in the 1871 and 1881 censuses and as a 'retired builder' in the 1891 census. Henry Maddern Jun seems to have started out as a joiner but by 1891 is recorded as an 'architect (student)'. In 1893 he married Elizabeth Polglase, a merchant's daughter, and in 1901 was working on his 'own account' as an architect and surveyor on St Mary's, Scilly. By 1902 Henry Maddern had returned to the mainland and set up business in Penzance at 26 Clarence Street and by 1909 he was well established at Morrab Road.[202] The earliest letter from Maddern to Mitchell (dated September 1909) is from the Morrab Road address. The letter is important in showing Maddern's role in questions relating to vernacular detailing, in this case tile-cladding.

I understand from Mr Gotch you wish the upright slating to be similar to some in the older part of Newlyn and have specified the method adopted by the old men with whom I worked when I was a lad. If that method of slating is of any service to you I shall be very pleased to give you full particulars of how we keep the same lap from eaves to ridge although the length of tail diminishes.[203]

The importance of using local, vernacular building methods underpinned the whole project of Wheal Betsy Cottage, as is clear from the correspondence between the clients, the architects and the builder. For example 'the whole of the stone to be used for the walling was to be from an approved local quarry', and the roof was to be in 'scantle slate from Delabole quarry.' Henry Maddern was also sympathetic to Gotch's wish to apply the Arts and Crafts principle of seeing the whole process from beginning to end to his own role as client. In the letter to Mitchell quoted above, Maddern refers to the 'apparently glaring differences' between local building terms and those to which Mitchell is accustomed but assures Mitchell that 'Mr Gotch will have no difficulty in following the builder in his operation…'. In fact, Gotch supervised the construction of the new house throughout although this was not fully appreciated by the builder, Mr Ed Pidwell, and towards the end of the contract there were some unpleasant recriminations.

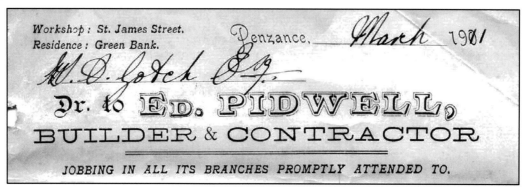

[200] Shears Archive: Ed Pidwell to TC Gotch, 4 May 1911.
[201] Tate Archive: Stanhope Forbes to Mrs Forbes, 2 May 1884 and 18 July 1886.
[202] Biographical information from censuses, parish registers and Kelly's Directories.
[203] Shears Archive: H Maddern, Penzance to Arnold Mitchell, 15 September 1909.

The builder

Edward Pidwell (b. 1851) was a Penzance man. Nothing is known about his father but his mother was Sarah James and his uncle George James was a mason. Edward was listed as a mason in the 1871, 1881 and 1901 censuses, and in the latter he was recorded as an employer. By 1906, he had a building and contracting business which operated from Green Bank, Penzance.[204]

Gotch was in contact with Pidwell from midsummer 1909 but could not finalise the contract until the building specifications, which were drawn up by Maddern, had been agreed by Mitchell. At the beginning of September, Pidwell was losing patience, and wrote: 'I must take a pair of villas close to where I am now building to keep my men and then I shall not be so well able to attend to yours if you do not decide until later and it's a dreadful place to work on top of that hill in the winter which is fast approaching'.[205] The deadline was met and the Memorandum of Agreement was signed by Thomas Cooper Gotch and Edward Pidwell in the presence of CJ Edmonds on 1 November 1909. Pidwell was to supply all materials and workmanship, and to build Wheal Betsy Cottage for £1169. But Pidwell was not an easy man as Gotch may have inferred from their first collision, not as sympathetic to the artist's close involvement as Henry Maddern seems to have been. At the end of the contract there was a clash of interest between the painstaking Gotch and the 'vernacular' Pidwell about the accounts, which was only resolved by Gotch taking Maddern's advice:

> In compliance with your instructions I have gone carefully through the a/c's and compared same with Mr. Pidwell's letters of explanation. In addition I have gone carefully through what he claims to have done to the roof, fireplaces etc. and has not charged. Having weighed the matter from both sides my advice to you is to put the work he has done but not charged for against the items which appear excessive and to settle the account. This is what I should do if the house were my own, the final difference would be so trivial that it would not be worth either going to arbitration or to court, and the worry you would endure seeing arbitrators or lawyers might upset your work for months.[206]

Wheal Betsy Cottage

In describing the architectural style of Wheal Betsy Cottage I have drawn upon two sources of evidence, physical and documentary. The physical evidence has been used to make comparisons with models found in architectural history and to draw conclusions. The documentary evidence comes from papers about the building of Wheal Betsy: the deeds of the house which include the 1908 Building Lease; architect's plans of the ground floor, second floor, roof and pipe work; specifications for masons', plumbers' and carpenters' work; memorandum of agreement between TC Gotch and Edward Pidwell; the final account from Pidwell, listing extra charges; and correspondence between the client, the architects and the builder. These items are in the Wheal Betsy Archive or in the Shears Archive.

Wheal Betsy Ground floor Plan
<<West East>>

The ground-floor plan (*right*) demonstrates the irregular and asymmetrical shape of Wheal Betsy Cottage. This was clearly an expression of Arts and Crafts utility and principle, and determined much of the internal arrangement of the house.

It is worth noting the four fireplaces on the ground floor. The chimney stack on the south side of the cottage served the parlour and the two south facing bedrooms above; the stack on the north side served the basement, lower hall, kitchen and dining room and had one dummy pot.

---

[204] Kelly's Directories 1906, 1910
[205] Shears Archive: Edward Pidwell to TC Gotch, 6 September 1911.
[206] Shears Archive: Henry Maddern to TC Gotch, 10 June 1911.

The porch was a reference to the vernacular symbolizing the welcome of the house. The porch is approached up three granite steps. The lower part of the door is a solid wood panel but the top is one of seven casement panels that together contain 185 small window panes. Another typical feature is the plain red tiled floor, reflecting the fashion in suburban houses of the time to avoid elaborate designs.

Left: Front porch. Right: Double door leading to the dining room (P.L.)

The broad two-panelled inner door is typical of the Queen Anne revival style, and a modification of six-panelled Georgian doors. It opens into the entrance hall, and its style is repeated in the two sets of wide double doors that lead to the dining room on the right and to the sitting room (parlour) on the left. These five doors are made of light coloured, highly polished mahogany and are complemented by the wooden floor. In an Arts and Crafts house, the only acceptable flooring was wood or stone. Wheal Betsy has narrow wooden floor boards made of 'red Norway', typical of Arts and Crafts interiors.

Window & Seat in Parlour, Wheal Betsy (PL)

An important feature is the wooden casement windows laid out in horizontal rows, with bay windows at the front of the house on all three floors. The windows are highly visible from outside, but it is from the inside that the value placed on light and air in an Arts and Crafts house becomes clear. In the early years of the Movement, sash windows were rejected because of their association with modern sheet glass, and the more vernacular wooden casement windows with many small panes of leaded glass were favoured. Mitchell used very small glass panes in the porch and in windows on the south-facing side of the house, with larger glass panes on the east and north sides. This pattern is present in the parlour and dining room and reflected in the bedrooms above.

The parlour at Wheal Betsy has seven eight-paned casements in the bay window in the east, and three twenty-four-paned casements in the south, making 128 panes all told. The natural light emphasises the use of simpler forms and colours that was a feature of Arts and Crafts interiors. Much of the interior of Wheal Betsy was painted white: Phyllis Gotch, who was in South Africa from 1911, would write and say, 'I wish I were in my dear white room at home'.[207] The window frames and sills and the window seat in the bay window are painted white. The lightness is reflected in the ceiling which is plastered and painted white with a simple picture rail fitted an inch or so below, and the whole spacious open plan room is enhanced by the golden mahogany doors.

---

[207] Wheal Betsy Archive: Phyllis Gotch, Hotel Victoria, Johannesburg to her parents, 7 August 1911

In the winter the large bay window of the Parlour was curtained off so that the fireplace became the focal point of the room. The fireplace was an important feature of Edwardian houses because despite a wealth of technological advances, the domestic house was still largely heated by coal fires. Typical Arts and Crafts fireplace designs were often elaborate and executed in brick, the fireplaces were large, often rounded and many had an inglenook feel. At Wheal Betsy, the architect opted for a much simpler style, probably influenced by the Gotches' taste for the more aesthetic side of Arts and Crafts values, which emphasised simplicity and an oriental flavour. The fireplace in the parlour was the most elaborate at Wheal Betsy (and very similar to one at Grove House Cottage), with a double over mantel on which the Gotches displayed their blue and white china; a collection which was influenced by the aesthetic movement, just as Morris and Whistler had been influenced in the 1870s.

Parlour, Wheal Betsy (P.L.)

For the fireplaces, the Gotches were probably influenced by MHB Baillie Scott, who favoured breadth and simplicity of effect and the avoidance of all patterns which startle when choosing tiles.[208] Tiling was popular for fireplace slips in Arts and Crafts houses and some of this was very fancy, but the Gotches could not afford the beautiful hand crafted tiles made by firms like Minton & Company from designs by such craftsmen as Walter Crane, and chose instead to get their fireplaces from a more mass-produced source, Bratt Colbran & Co, the Heaped Fire Company. For the parlour they chose 'a hammered brass interior eighteen inch heaped fire 24½ x 36¼, an all brass hob, a slabbed surround in 'Grey Lustre' tiles to show twelve inches all round, and a hearth to suit. The price was £9-0-10d.'

The Fireplace in the Lower Hall (above left) has a single pine shelf with a white painted wood surround and green mottled 2 x 2 inch tiles with hearth to match. Inside this surround (above right) is the Bratt Colbran 15 inch heaped fire with the makers name and number on the firebricks and grate, and a copper and black hob. (P.L.)

---

[208] *The Studio* VI No 31, October 1895: 101-107.

Although the hall, the dining room and the drawing room were on one level, the Gotches had to descend to the lower hall to get access to the pantry and kitchen; down another level for the cloakroom and toilet; and down yet another level to a small landing and the staircase leading to the basement room. Access to the pantry was through a wide swinging door that led to another door to the kitchen where there was a kitchen range with a slate hearth; the architect had specified that 'in the rooms with no tiled hearths they are to be Delabole slate 1½' thick.' From the kitchen another step down led to the scullery where there was a back door with a flight of granite steps into the garden. There was a dresser cupboard in the pantry, and a dresser and large built-in cupboard in the kitchen and drain boards in both pantry and scullery (carpenter's specifications). There were three lavatories in the house and although the original specifications listed earth closets, this was changed to water closets, one of the reasons for Pidwell's increased bill.[209] Although the original intention was to build a store-room under the house, Gotch must have changed his mind as the possibilities of the room became apparent. Floors were lowered and the fireplace opening enlarged to make room for the 'green briquette fireplace, 18' heaped fire, armour bright hob, pine shelf, copper and black hob, and hearth to suit'.

Basement at Wheal Betsy. Left: Bay window. Right: Internal feature (P.L)

The basement room is an interesting feature of the house with two large windows, a small lobby and an outside door. It has a wooden ceiling and rafters and a narrow planked floor. The work must have been done by the carpenter, FR Mudge, whose name is engraved on the underside of the floor of the Parlour and dated 10 June 1911. The basement was used by Phyllis from 1931-1937; the Gotches must have felt about the basement very much like Gertrude Jekyll did about the oak gallery in her house.

Thanks to my good architect, who conceived the place in exactly such a form as I had desired, but could not have described, and to the fine old carpenter who worked to his drawings in an entirely sympathetic manner, I may say that it is a good example of how English oak should be used in an honest building, whose only pretension is to be of sound work done with the right intention, of material used according to the capability of its nature and the purpose designed with due regard to beauty of proportion and simplicity of effort.[210]

Postscript: The Wheal Betsy lease was for ninety-nine years from 29 September 1908. When Gotch died in 1931 the lease passed to Caroline and, on her death in 1945, to Phyllis. Phyllis' daughter Patricia inherited the lease on the death of her mother in 1963 and she purchased the freehold of Wheal Betsy the following year. The house was sold to her daughter Miranda in 1974 and to the present owners in 1996.

---

[209] Shears Archive: Pidwell to TC Gotch,13 October 1909
[210] Jekyll: 25

12. Onward Christian Soldiers

Anthony Noonan

The aim of this chapter is to identify the various Christian denominations which have been active in Penwith in the twentieth century, and then to trace how the individual elements in this cluster fared. It is a complex story, and I hope that the picture portrayed is not an unworthy caricature.

Christianity seems to have made its first serious impact in West Cornwall with the arrival of Irish missionaries between 500 and 550 AD, although there is evidence of at least some earlier Christian activity in Penwith, in the Carnsew slab in Hayle and the chi-rho stone at Phillack.[211] The Saxon conquest in the tenth century and the Norman conquest of the eleventh century saw the Cornish Church becoming more strongly linked to the rest of Britain, and the building of many fine churches on ancient sites. The Reformation of the 1540s banned the Latin Mass and the use of the Cornish language in church, leading to the Western Rebellion of 1549. The Cornish army was defeated and the Catholic religion repressed. In the battles and subsequent subjugation it is estimated that 5000 Cornishmen died[212]—an amazing ten per cent of the population. The Toleration Act of 1689 permitted dissenters to worship in the manner of their choice (though not Catholics), and thus began to pave the way for a diverse Christian culture to develop over the next three centuries. The twentieth century provided many challenges to the Christian community.

Methodists

John Wesley began the first of his thirty-two visits to Cornwall on 29 August 1743 and set up his headquarters in St Ives, where there was already a Methodist Society. By 1851, the ecclesiastical census returns revealed that 65 per cent of those attending Sunday worship in Cornwall went to a Methodist chapel. Methodism remained the most influential religious group in twentieth-century Penwith, and beneath that umbrella there have been quite a number of sub-denominations. Prior to 1907 the list comprised: Bible Christian, Methodist New Connexion, Primitive, United Methodist Free Churches, Wesleyan and Wesleyan Free Churches. Following an earlier partial reunion of 1907, 1932 saw a process which brought all the groups together except the Wesleyan Reform Union. The St Just Free Methodist Church, which is still part of the Wesleyan Reform Union, chose independence. An example of the schisms was that prior to 1923, Penzance had chapels for six different Methodist denominations.[213] However, on the ground, the reunions did not always proceed smoothly or quickly. As Easton points out, chapels in Penzance which

Revivalist Meeting at St Clements Wesleyan Chapel, Mousehole 1912
Courtesy Margaret Perry

joined in 1907 to form the United Methodist Union continued in separate circuits for the twenty-five years following and with the addition of the two former Wesleyan and Primitive circuits continued to do so until the 1950s. A similar situation occurred in St Ives where, even today, there are two circuits, one of them being that of the former Primitive Methodists, now with only one chapel[214]

---

[211] Thomas: 5.
[212] Rose-Troup: 40.
[213] Easton: 61.
[214] Easton: 25.

Amalgamations, decreasing membership and attendance, population losses caused by the severe decline of mining in the St Just area at the beginning of the period, and the economics of repair and maintenance to ageing buildings were all reasons why chapel closures would be an inevitable part of the century. (Usually when chapels have not been viable they have been sold and the congregations encouraged to join with other churches.) So it is perhaps surprising that the membership of the Penwith circuits for 1990 (1689 members) and 2000 (1688 members) are virtually identical.[215] Possibly this is a sign of a corner turned. Another surprise is that the attendance for 1990 (2415) was actually higher than 1980(2335). The former Methodist superintendent, Rev Ian Haile, suggests that this was because the evangelical John Horner was particularly successful in Penzance in 1990: people travelled great distances to hear him. Ten years later, in 2000, the weekly attendance figure dipped to 1344, a decline of 44 per cent in ten years.

Wesley Reform Unionists

This branch of Methodism, founded in the mid-nineteenth century, stayed outside the reunion processes of 1907 and 1932. In St Just it has a church which dates back to 1860. For much of the twentieth century there was also a small chapel at Carnyorth.

Anglicans

The Anglican Church in Cornwall emerged from the religious turmoil of the Tudor years. Cornwall remained part of the Exeter Diocese and in many ways went through lean times for much of the

Rev Bernard Walke at St Hilary (Courtesy Morrab Library)

eighteenth and nineteenth centuries. A new beginning was possible with the establishment of a Cornish Diocese in 1877. With its own Bishop and a new Cathedral, the Diocese of Truro was to embark on a lively and re-invigorated twentieth century. In this the Penwith Deanery was to play its full part. One of the tensions to play itself out during the century was the differing views of the Protestant and Anglo-Catholic wings. Most of the Bishops of Truro during the twentieth century were Anglo-Catholics, but they steered a prudent course designed to promote harmony.

In 1932 the parish of St Hilary witnessed dramatic scenes of conflict whilst under ministry of Bernard Walke. He was a very enthusiastic Anglo-Catholic of remarkable talents: for example, in 1926, the BBC broadcast the St Hilary Players performing the first of his plays for All Souls and the Nativity; he founded an orphanage in a one-time public house; and his church had been gradually enriched with painted choir-stalls, pictures, statues and several stone altars. A number of locals did not care for this, and they won a ruling at the Consistory Court to remove certain objects; but Walke refused to comply. Protestant action was decided upon and on 8 August 1932 a group arrived at St Hilary, some in cars and others in a coach from Plymouth. They tricked their way into the church and with the use of crowbars and hammers broke down statues, pictures and sections of the high altar. Walke renewed the things destroyed and the church took on again something of its former beauty for the time being.

Whilst shifts may have taken place over the years the following parishes can be categorised as following the Anglo-Catholic tradition during the twentieth century: St Hilary, St Ives, St Elwin (Hayle), St Erth, Marazion, St Buryan, St Mary's (Penzance), Carbis Bay, St Peter's (Newlyn), and St Paul's (Penzance). Towards the end of the century, one of the main issues to emerge was the ordination of women. In Penwith as elsewhere, it was controversial. The sensitivities of the opponents were respected by allowing dissenting parishes to adopt one or more of the following resolutions:

a) No woman priest can officiate within the parish

b) The incumbent must be a man

---

[215] NB however that membership figures are always somewhat lower than attendance figures.

c) A parish could petition the bishop that episcopal oversight must be provided by a bishop who has not ordained a woman

In Cornwall, Bishop Michael Ball recommended a 'No Resolution' approach and gave the assurance that he would not appoint a female priest to a parish against its will. St Hilary and St Ives adopted (a) and (b) whilst St Just went further and also adopted (c). The remaining twenty-four parishes followed the Bishop's advice. Reputedly opposition to the ordination of women has increased nationally since 1994, but in Cornwall, and in Penwith, it has decreased.

Faced with the economic realities of maintaining three churches in Penzance, St Paul's was closed in 1998. This was an understandably painful experience for people who had developed a loyalty to their own church. It seems a remarkable achievement that by the end of the century there were still twenty-six Anglican churches in Penwith, enjoying a very high standard of care and maintenance with the majority open during the day.

Roman Catholics

Three hundred years after the Reformation, Fr William Young, a charismatic Irishman of great talents and a driving determination to establish a Catholic Mission to Cornwall, arrived from Dublin via Bodmin in 1840 and set up a Penzance Mission.[216] Much of the money for the new Church of the Immaculate Conception of Our Lady was donated from Ireland. From 1894 to 1939 (one third of the twentieth century), Canon Bernard Wade was the parish priest.[217] During his forty years in Penzance numbers increased with many new families moving in, particularly after the First World War.

A Catholic church was also opened in St Ives in 1908, and in 1958 a former Baptist church was acquired in Hayle. From 1975, a Saturday mass was said at St Just, where the Anglicans made their parish church available in a gesture of ecumenism. Families of Italian and Polish miners working at Geevor mine were prominent in the congregation.

One unexpected visitor to Penzance in 1920 was the great Irishman, Archbishop Mannix of Melbourne. He had been in the USA sharing platforms with Eamon de Valera speaking for the Irish Independence cause. Then on a voyage to Ireland, a British destroyer intercepted his ship. He was forcibly removed by the British authorities who were unhappy with the prospect of him landing in Ireland during troublesome times. He was landed at Penzance, and said mass in the church before been taken to London by train.

The post-second world war period was a time of consolidation. Church attendances declined in the last decade or so of the century. In Penzance for example it dropped from an average of 376 in 1992 to 294 in 2000, a loss of 22 per cent.

Salvationists

William Booth, the founder of the Salvation Army had a strong relationship with Penwith, similar to John Wesley's. Prior to his departure from the Methodist New Connexion, he was invited to Cornwall and held a very energetic evangelising campaign, which was particularly successful in St Just, St Ives, Hayle, and Penzance. In the early 1860s, the Booths were staying in Penzance where their fifth child, Herbert, was born. The first Salvation Army citadels in Penwith were inaugurated in Hayle and St Ives in 1879. Penzance followed in 1881.The first half of the twentieth century was a time of growth with citadels being established in St Just, Marazion, Newlyn and Mousehole. These smaller ones did not survive but the three original citadels enjoyed an active life throughout the century and are still going strong. The founding ethos of the Army, to serve the spiritual and welfare needs of the most deprived members of society, remained the Army's mission in Penwith throughout. It was towards the end of the century that it undertook one of its most exciting initiatives. Based at its Penzance Citadel it established the Breakfast Project along with the churches in Penzance and Newlyn. In practice the project is run by the Army and assisted by volunteers from the various churches. Three hundred and sixty-five days a year from 07:00 to 09:00, cooked breakfasts along with toast, tea and coffee are served to the homeless in a warm, friendly and non-proselytising atmosphere.

---

[216] An earlier attempt in 1838 had failed.
[217] Smith: 5. Fr Wade was appointed Missionary Rector in 1898.

Founder's Visit. General Booth at Penzance Station, 11 August 1909
(Courtesy Morrab Library)

In common with other denominations, attendances have fallen during the latter part of the century. However, in 1999 the approximate average attendance at the three citadels still came to 115 people. A distinguishing characteristic of the Army is that women have been admitted into the ministry since its inception. Currently, three out of four of its ministers in Penwith are female.

Plymouth Brethren

This denomination, also known as the Christian Brethren, started as a little Evangelical group in Dublin in 1827, having seceded from the (Anglican) Church of Ireland. John Darby of Trinity College Dublin is recognised as its founder. In 1830 he visited and spread his ideas in the West Country and found Plymouth to be the most receptive city. A number of groups were established in and around the city on both sides of the Tamar. In the late nineteenth century, a Gospel Hall was established in St Ives. In Penzance, they used various places in the town, latterly the former synagogue in New Street. This Hall closed in the 1960s.

The St Ives congregation subscribes to the 'Kelly' or 'Open' interpretation as opposed to that of the Exclusive Brethren. The latter have been heavily criticised for being rigid and intolerant of non-members often causing conflict and pain within families. The Brethren are very much focussed on Biblical truths and the Trinity. So far they have not changed the rule that women should keep their heads covered and not speak at meetings. In recent years they have seen membership and attendance decline. At the end of the century weekly attendance had dipped from eighty to about twenty-five. They have practical co-operation with other faith groups and meet at Gospel Outreach where ministers from other denominations address them.[218]

Quakers

George Fox, founder of the Religious Society of Friends, first visited Cornwall in 1656, spending a night in Marazion. The early Quakers were regarded as a threat to the state and, along with other Dissenters, suffered significant persecution. Fox himself spent a year in Launceston Gaol on contrived charges.

The Friends Meeting House at Marazion (1688) is a building of great character and simplicity. Towards the end of the nineteenth century, however, there were few Friends locally, and it fell out of use until after World War I, having been let out to the Salvation Army for about ten years at the turn of

---

[218] Interview with Church Elder, Billy Perkin, 20 December 2006.

the century. By the early sixties the number of the Marazion Friends had dwindled again to about five, who in winter would huddle around a stove for their meeting. However, in the latter decades numbers steadily increased to such an extent that the Marazion Meeting House was no longer big enough, and in 1996 it was necessary to form a new group in Penzance. By the end of 1999 the typical Marazion attendance was twenty-five adults plus children with a ten to fifteen Friends meeting in Penzance.

The Religious Society of Friends is certainly different from other faith groups. There are no priests, no rituals nor structured services. Friends sit in silence in communion with one another; after a time someone may feel inspired to stand up and speak briefly—in their own words or from the Bible or some other book. Quakers are well known for their activity on social issues; above all they say that following the teachings of Jesus means that you must rule out war and violence as a way of solving problems. The Society is egalitarian in nature with its elders being elected for a period of three years. Women have complete equality and sexual orientation or practice is no bar to being an elder.[219]

Baptists

At the start of the twentieth century there were Baptist churches in Penzance and Hayle. There was a Strict Baptist Church in Sennen which opened in 1902. It is unclear when it closed but the building was still standing with its tiny gallery in 1951.[220] The Penzance church received its most famous visitor in 1984 when Prime Minister Thatcher attended a service to commemorate the lives of two young boys missing at sea, presumed drowned. In 1986 the church celebrated its 150th anniversary under the leadership of the Rev Hywel Roberts who has been its Minister since the early 1970s. It is a mark of his leadership and of the vitality of the Penzance congregation that their attendance numbers have been sustained at about eighty persons during these years.

Apostolics

There is one apostolic congregation in Penwith based in Newlyn and dating back to the 1930s. Previously there was another congregation in Penzance but this ceased to function in the 1960s. The Church is a Pentecostal denomination and traces its roots to the 1905 Welsh Revival.

Zion Congregationalists

This denomination might claim to be the oldest non-conformist group in Penwith, and traces its foundation back to 1662 in St Ives, although there is evidence that that group had lapsed by 1775, when Selina Hastings, Countess of Huntingdon, visited the town and established a mission which the remnants of the independent chapel joined.[221] The present chapel there (1804) is built on an old fish-house and salt-cellar, and for many years it was the 'Zion Congregational Countess of Huntingdon's Connexion'. Perhaps uniquely, it held joint membership of the Connexion and the Congregationalists from 1823 to 1971, when it resigned from the Congregational Confederation.[222] Despite an ageing and declining membership, it survived the century with a lasting and deep attachment to the Countess.

Congregationalists

In 1707 a Congregational meeting house was also built on Market Jew Street, Penzance, and was active for the next 250 years.[223] In 1959, another meeting house was opened in an ambitious attempt to serve the new housing estate at Alverton on the edge of Penzance, but only nine members enrolled.

Meanwhile the building at Market Jew Street was in an appalling condition. No minister could be appointed for the now combined Alverton and Penzance congregations—probably because Penzance had the worst fund-raising performance in Cornwall. There was even a suggestion in 1967 that they share a minister with Zion St Ives but this came to nothing. In 1968 there were a number of resignations and the final blow came with the closure of both chapels in 1969.[224]

---

[219] Anon: 1.

[220] Isaac: 235.

[221] The information in this paragraph comes from Noall; thanks to Cedric Appleby for pointing this out to me.

[222] Densham.

[223] Ball: 8.

[224] CCC: CRO X682/40; X682/21/10/66; X682/45; X682/45. Church minutes end in 1969.

Fishermen's Mission

The Royal National Mission to Deep-Sea Fishermen in Newlyn is very much a twentieth-century story. It can trace its humble origins back to 1902 when a Mrs Tonkin rented a cottage near the harbour as a recreation room for fishermen.

In 1911 the present splendid mission building was opened. Nothing much that has happened in Penwith has not occurred in St Ives. They had their own Mission in what is now the Museum building. With the rundown of the fishing industry in the town, this Mission was closed in the 1960s and its needs along with those of the other Cornish ports are looked after by Newlyn. A distinctive feature of the Mission nationally is that it is truly inter-denominational, drawing its ministers from Anglican, Methodist and Baptist persuasions.

Jehovah's Witnesses

This group originated in the USA and established a presence here in 1907 when it held its first meetings in Penzance, led by a Mr Proust. Its members are now served by a rather splendid Kingdom Hall which opened at St Erth in 1997 to serve the Penzance and Hayle congregations. A core belief is that God's Kingdom has Jesus as King; they claim to have restored first-century Christianity. Unlike other Penwith denominations they reject the creed of the Trinity, eternal torment in Hell and the immortality of the soul.

Christian Spiritualists

This congregation established a church in Penzance in 1960. Its Minister up to 1994 was Elsie Dickens (a direct descendant of Charles Dickens). They believe in the Bible and the traditional Christian message, but what makes them distinctive is their claim to have proof that life continues after death and that the spirits of the departed contact the living.

Towards the end of the century numbers attending remained steady at an average of 25. The composition of the congregation changed, however, from being predominantly elderly and female to include many more young people and males. In addition to a minister, healers and mediums have key roles in the church.

Independents

The significant number of either independent or semi-autonomous congregations illustrates Penwith's Christian diversity. Many of them are relatively new, three having appeared in the 1990s. They share certain characteristics: they are evangelical; their founders felt a calling from God to make a distinctive independent contribution; they attract a mainly English congregation, in their thirties and forties; they are born-again Christians; and they have a steadily increasing membership.

The vision of the **Shekinah Christian Church**, Penzance (1992) is to know the palpable presence of God in themselves and to work for the transformation of the community. **Christian Fellowship Church on the Rock**, Ludgvan (1994)has as its defining goal to stick closely to Bible teaching; it is charismatic, sharing gifts of the Holy Spirit. **Elim Pentecostal**, St Ives (1998), believes that the gifts of the Holy Spirit are available today, to be used today.

Earlier established Independents include: **Carnhell Green Fellowship** (1968), which started with a small group of people who met on Sunday evenings for Bible studies. Numbers grew and a modern church was built. It is a non-denominational group of born-again believers. By the end of the century, its average Sunday attendance was about 80. **Connor Down Evangelical Free Church** was originally a Methodist Free Church but in 1982 the church's property was conveyed to the present trustees and the church is now run on a completely independent basis. Average attendance in 1999 was about 20. **Alverton Evangelical Free Church**, Penzance (1974) adheres to the 1689 Baptist Confession of Faith and prior to 1974 was linked to Clarence Street Baptists. It is solidly evangelical.

Questionnaire and Survey Analysis

For the purpose of this research, eighteen ministers or church elders were interviewed using a pre-designed questionnaire.[225] The aim was to include one representative from each denomination; in fact fifteen denominations were represented, plus two that are inter-denominational or non-denominational. Each interviewee agreed that in general, attendances at places or worship had declined since the 1960s. Attendances had increased at the Quakers (Marazion and Penzance), Elim Pentecostal (St Ives), Carnhell Green Meeting, Church on the Rock (Ludgvan), Jehovah's Witness and Shekinah Christian Church (Penzance). The Baptists (Penzance) and Apostolic Church (Newlyn) had more or less maintained their positions. Diminished attendances occurred with the Methodists and Anglicans but at the end of the century over half of church attendances were still at one or the other of these two main players. The Roman Catholics, Salvation Army, Alverton Free Church, Plymouth Brethren, and Zion Congregational Church all sustained lower attendances in the latter decades. The interviewees were asked to indicate opinions as to the reasons for falling church attendances. Several were not prepared to adopt a 'tick the box' approach. The table below presents the results.

Opinion Survey of Ministers and Church Elders on Declining Church Attendances						
Reasons	Strongly agree	Agree	Undecided	Disagree	Strongly disagree	Irrelevant
The rise of science	2	3	2	2		2
Secularism	7	5				
Availability of alternative activities (TV, sport, shopping etc.)	4	7				
Looser family ties (divorce, etc)	4	6	1			
Gender revolution resulting in loss of young females from patriarchal churches	2	3	5	1		
Unsympathetic media	3	4	1	3		

Other suggested reasons included: an ageing church membership not attracting the young; reduction of deference; weak leadership without passionate beliefs; younger people leaving Cornwall; failure of churches to move with the times and attract people; wars; and apathy towards organised religion due to failure of churches to grapple with real issues.

While responses tended to support the thesis that an increasingly secular society, with looser family and community ties, has contributed to a decline in attendance—and while in addition, Sundays now offer many competing activities, including entertainment, sport and shopping—in spite of all this, the average total Sunday attendance at eighty-three places of Christian worship in Penwith at the end of the century was nearly four thousand people. Generally speaking, the role of women had been enhanced. Nine of the seventeen faith groups accepted women ministers. The same was not true of practising homosexuals. Only Quakers said that a gay person could be elected as an Elder. Over the century it is clear that many prejudices had been broken down: the different denominations get on much better. By 2000 there were quite a few examples of cooperation, none more impressive than the Churches in Penzance and Newlyn Breakfast for the Homeless Project, led by the Salvation Army.

The non-Cornish ministers were asked had they found it different working in Penwith. Responses included: 'Cornish people take a while to get to know'; 'It was very hard coming here, it was like stepping back 100 years'; 'Before I was a Minister we came to live on the Lizard and no one spoke to us for six months'; 'Cornish are similar to people in other rural areas'; 'In Cornwall there is more respect for Clergy'; 'There is a natural reluctance to trust anyone or anything that comes from over the Tamar'; 'St Ives is quite parochial' and 'Doing it drekly is reality not a joke'.

---

[225] Questionnaire based on Brown CG: 224-69.

Places of Worship & Attendances (Autumn 1999)				
Faith group	No. of churches /chapels	Usual Sunday attendance	Group present through the century	Year formed
Methodist	35	1344	✓	
Anglican*	26	1246*	✓	
Roman Catholic	3	431	✓	
Salvation Army	3	115	✓	
Quaker	2	35	✓	
Plymouth Brethren	1	25	✓	
Baptist	1	80	✓	
Wesley Reform Union	1	30	✓	
Zion Congregational**Error! Bookmark not defined.**	1	7	✓	
Apostolic	1	40		1930
Fishermen's Mission	1	35		1902
Carnhell Green	1	80		1968
Connor Downs Evangelical	1	12		1982
Elim Pentecostal	1	40		1998
Shekinah	1	90		1992
Church on the Rock	1	30		1994
Alverton Free Church	1	20		1974
Jehovah's Witness	1	215		1907
Christian Spiritualist	1	25		1960
Total	83	3900		
(* 1999 and 2000 figures not available. 2001 figure used)				

Conclusions

The twentieth century, particularly the latter part, was a period of enormous social change. Secular legislation, which decriminalised homosexuality, legalised abortion, allowed easier divorces and liberalised Sunday shopping were all significant influences for a changing society. In addition, Penwith was subject to population changes that from the 1970s saw the increasing influence of English people, second homes, and the decline of traditional working-class industries. By 1999, approximately 10 per cent of housing units in Penwith were holiday or second homes. The decline in working-class culture has almost certainly affected Methodism, Roman Catholicism and the Salvation Army more negatively than Anglicanism and some other groups including the Quakers. Towards the end of the century, Anglicanism was steadily catching up the Methodists in the attendance league-table and predictably overtook it in the early part of the twenty-first century. Traditional older denominations including the Wesley Reform Union, Zion Congregational, and Plymouth Brethren survived the Century but suffered losses. The Apostolic and Baptists seemed to do rather well in keeping up their numbers. Furthermore, there are eight congregations which can be described as 'independents'. All can be categorized as evangelical and the three latest additions are enjoying significant growth.

The fact that there are nearly four thousand people attending a total of eighty-three places of Christian worship each Sunday hardly spells the end of Christianity. Increased ecumenical co-operation is also a healthy development. Most Penwith Christians share core beliefs. They believe in the Trinity, that Jesus died on the cross to save us, and that the Bible is the inspired word of God. What divides Christians from each other seemed less important at the end of the century than at the beginning. The story of Penwith's twentieth-century Christianity is the story of many thousands of believers. In spite of differences, basically they chose to bear witness to the same values and beliefs, which were introduced into Cornwall along the banks of the Hayle Estuary fifteen hundred years ago.

13. Early Motoring in West Penwith

Margaret Perry

Before the arrival of motorised vehicles most roads in West Cornwall were narrow and winding, deeply rutted, muddy in wet weather and extremely dusty when dry. These roads would have developed from ancient track-ways linking farms, villages and the coastal ports. By the mid nineteenth century changes were taking place, major roads in many areas were affected by the coming of the railway, a fast means of transporting both goods and people. Travellers would have found rail travel faster and more comfortable than a coach or travelling by sea, this last the more usual way to undertake longer journeys and to transport goods to and from Cornwall.

During the eighteenth and nineteenth centuries Cornwall was at the forefront of experiments in powering self-propelled vehicles on the road. By the 1820s technical improvements made steam motoring more practicable. However, there was concern over damage to roads and bridges, with risk of boiler explosion and injury to people and property. Turnpike trusts, which controlled the main highways, discriminated against such vehicles because they damaged the road surface. While a horse-drawn coach would be charged a toll of 3/- (15p), a steam carriage would be obliged to pay £2. Then, in 1865, Parliament stepped in with the *Locomotive Act*, which restricted the permissible speed for all self propelled vehicles to no more than 4 mph in the country and 2 mph in towns. Vehicles had to have a crew of two, with a third person walking in front displaying a red flag or, at night, a red lantern. It was an impossible situation and, although interest in this country did not lessen, most development in petrol-driven vehicles at this time was on the Continent, in France and Germany, and also in America.

In addition to steam vehicles, increasing numbers of bicycles were using the roads and in 1878 the *Highways and Locomotives Amendment Act* allowed for the setting up of Highways, Bridges and Roads Committees in each county. Cornwall duly elected a committee in October of that year at Quarter sessions and meetings were held in Lostwithiel.[226] At first mainly concerned with setting up an administrative structure, the committee asked the Clerks of the several Unions of the county to furnish approximate mileage of Turnpike Roads and Highways within their respective areas and asked if they were desirous in addition to their other duties to exercise the functions of a Highway Board. It must have come as no surprise when it was reported that there was a 'general disinclination' in the county to comply with this request. A Surveyor was appointed for each of the two divisions of the county, Eastern and Western. They were required to frame bye-laws for the future consideration of the committee. The last turnpike trust ended in 1885, turnpikes became main roads and half the expense of maintaining these was to be met out of the county rate. Power was given to the committee to declare an ordinary highway to be a main road and this led to a number of requests. In 1880 an application was made for parts of the roads at Chyandour and Newlyn Green to be declared main roads. It was decided not to entertain the proposal at this time, and throughout the rest of the decade Penzance applied at each meeting to have certain roads designated without success. At last, in 1890 the Committee approved roads totalling 74 miles, 2 furlongs, 2 poles in the Western Division, which included:

- Madron Local Board- the roads from Marazion to Penzance and Alverton to Buryas Bridge
- Board of Gulval- the road from Long Rock to Ponsandane
- Board of Paul- the road from Buryas Bridge to the bottom of Drift Hill

In 1894 the Committee finally agreed to make a contribution towards the maintenance and repair of the disputed mile from Chyandour to Alverton but refused to agree to the Newlyn Green road being made a main road.[227]

The *Locomotives on the Highway Act* which became known as the *Emancipation Act* was introduced in 1895. This Act abolished the red flag requirement of 1865, which had been partially lifted in 1878 for vehicles under three tonnes, and the speed limit was raised to a maximum of 14 mph. In the event most local authorities restricted speed to under 12 mph and a lower limit could be set. At last cars could take to the roads of Britain. The introduction of the Act was commemorated by a celebratory run from London to Brighton in which thirty-two vehicles took part, both steam and

---

[226] Cornwall Record Office (CRO) CC/1/5/1
[227] CRO: CC/1/5/3 Highways, Bridges and Main Roads Committee Minutes

petrol-driven, including some motorised bicycles. This was possibly half the cars then in the country. Not all the drivers completed the journey and some finished by train. The London to Brighton run was to become an annual event in 1927.

1897 Daimler twin-cylinder, 6hp Wagonette, pictured in Penzance, believed to be the car driven by Henry Sturmey
(Courtesy Morrab Library)

The Daimler Motor Company had been established in Germany in 1885 and was quickly off the mark in Britain, starting production at Coventry in 1896, less than a year after the introduction of the Emancipation Act. Henry Sturmey, a pioneer of motoring in Britain, was a director of the Daimler Company and editor of the motoring magazine *Autocar* established in 1895. In 1897 he fulfilled his ambition of driving from one end of Britain to the other, a journey that had become popular with cyclists. His companion on the journey was a young engineer, Richard Ashley, a Daimler employee working in the motor-testing shop of the company. Not a driver, he took 'a few lessons in driving a day or two before the start, so as to be competent to take a turn at the helm.' He also got together duplicates of any parts which might be needed on the journey. Henry Sturmey wrote an account of the journey and this was published in *Autocar* in 1898. The motor consumed 67½ gallons of petrol for the 929 miles from John o'Groats to Land's End. The average travelling speed, taken throughout, worked out at a shade less than 10 mph, the actual travelling time being 93½ hours. In his account of the journey Henry Sturmey described his arrival in Penzance and later at Land's End:

> *As we reached the town and commenced the long ascent, our ride became a triumphal procession. The elevated footways, as well as the road, were crowded with sightseers. Every window had its occupants, and a perfect roar of applause greeted us as we progressed...The very steep winding hill into the centre of the town was simply packed with people and, apparently, all the available police force of the town engaged in keeping a narrow way for our progress. After a few minutes stoppage we again set forth on the last ten miles of our journey, accompanied by a number of cyclists. The first five miles were exceedingly rough, as well as very steep and very muddy, the gradients being mainly in the ascendant, and then having reached top ground, we ran along over roads which were fairly level, and although better in surface, still bad and narrow...we drew up at the Land's End Hotel at 4.35pm, with a score of 929 miles to our credit, and the journey successfully accomplished.*

Henry Sturmey wrote a detailed account of this journey, which was full of incident, and described his reception in towns and villages throughout Cornwall.[228] Although some of the spectators would have seen a steam-driven vehicle before, it is likely, at this early date, that few would have seen a petrol-driven car. The *Cornishman* newspaper reporter was less enthusiastic than most. In a brief account he commented:

> *...Hundreds crowded the streets of Penzance on Tuesday afternoon, and great excitement prevailed when the machine hove in sight, with three passengers on board, and proceeded swiftly and very easily up Market-Jew Street. A stop was made for a few minutes outside the Western hotel and admiring crowds endeavoured to sniff as much ill smell of benzoline and hear as much whirring of the works as time allowed them...[229]*

The technical details given in his report were taken from a card that Henry Sturmey had prepared, anticipating that he would be asked innumerable questions at every stop. He called these 'save trouble

---

[228] Hough. For full bibliographical details, see the Bibliography on pp. 113-116.
[229] *Cornishman,* October 1897

cards' and the information given reveals the lack of knowledge of the motor-car at this date. There are twenty statements of fact under the heading 'What is it?' including:

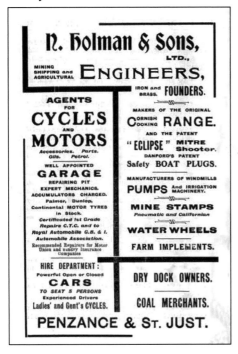

Advertisement from Rodda's Penzance Almanack, 1913

- It is an autocar, some people call it a motor-car
- It is worked by a petroleum motor
- No, it can't explode – there is no boiler.

With a number of companies starting production, and the option of importing a motor from France or Germany, interest in possessing a car intensified, but only those with sufficient money to meet the high cost of the customised, hand-built vehicles could hope to own one. Sturmey's Coventry-Daimler with a 4 hp German engine cost £370; in that same year (1897) a row of newly built granite houses in Newlyn sold for £200 each, and older properties were available for less than half that sum.

There were already a small number of steam-driven vehicles in Cornwall and over the next few years petrol-driven cars started to arrive, S.Hicks & Son of Truro claim to have sold the first motor-car in Cornwall in May 1900. Samuel Hicks took over an established coach-building firm in River Street in 1876 and the firm continued in business until 1976. They had started dealing in Humber bicycles when cycling became popular and when Humber pioneered the manufacture of motorised vehicles Samuel Hicks placed his first order for a car with that firm: the Humber Phaeton 3½ hp took two and a half days to complete the 270-mile journey from Coventry to Truro, William Hicks having travelled to Coventry to accompany the engineer delivering the car. He taught William to drive during the journey, and in his turn William taught the purchaser of the car, a Mr Powell.[230]

Following the arrival of the motor-car garages sprang up like mushrooms. At first they had a number of descriptive names including motor stable or shed, but gradually the term 'garage' was used to describe a place where cars were kept. In time the term became used to describe the whole package, the workshop aspect and the hiring and sale of cars. These early garages developed from other businesses: posting establishments, blacksmiths, cycle shops and coach builders. This was the case with two early contenders for first garage in Penzance, N. Holman & Sons Ltd and S. R. Taylor & Sons Ltd both engineering firms. Many hotels were quick to offer accommodation for motorists' cars, as well as inspection pits, qualified engineers and petrol, alongside the usual stabling and posting facilities. Supplies of fuel oil were uncertain—when Sturmey drove to Land's End in 1897 he solved the problem by despatching fuel by rail to collect at stations along the route.

From 1900 all containers for conveying or keeping petrol were limited to a two-gallon capacity. This changed with the start of the First World War when cans were at a premium for military use. It was at this time that the first petrol-pump appeared, improving the fuel-distribution network. These were expensive to install, requiring a 500-gallon fuel-tank to be sunk below the pump and filled at intervals by deliveries from a petrol tanker. The petrol-pump which for many years stood at the front of the Great Grimsby Coal, Salt and Tanning Company premises on the Harbour Road at Newlyn was installed in 1924.[231] The first purpose-built roadside filling-station appeared in 1919. In time petrol companies paid for the installation of tanks and pumps on credit, thus tying garages to their fuel contracts for long periods of time.

A significant piece of legislation came into force in 1903 when the *Motor-car Act* was introduced. This Act required all vehicles to be registered from 1 January 1904; licences were issued at a cost of £1 and registration marks had to be clearly displayed. Driving licences, for identification purposes only, were also introduced and cost five shillings (25p) from post offices. Registration numbers were

[230] Weeks
[231] CRO: DC Pen 296

allocated by county: London was given the letter A, the first registration letters for Cornwall being AF. Used for the first 9,999 vehicles registered AF did not run out until 1924 when the letters RL came into use, followed in 1929 with the prefix CV. This was completed in 1932, giving some indication of the rapidly accelerating build-up of road users in the latter years.

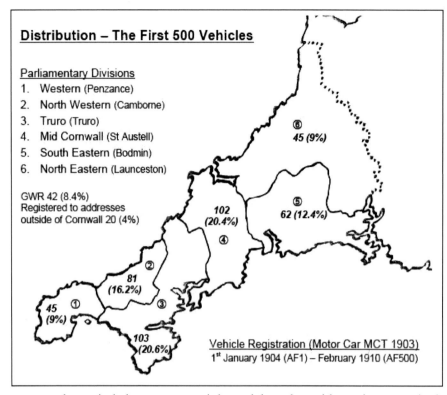

Distribution – The First 500 Vehicles

Parliamentary Divisions
1. Western (Penzance)
2. North Western (Camborne)
3. Truro (Truro)
4. Mid Cornwall (St Austell)
5. South Eastern (Bodmin)
6. North Eastern (Launceston)

GWR 42 (8.4%)
Registered to addresses
outside of Cornwall 20 (4%)

⑥ 45 (9%)

102 (20.4%)

⑤ 62 (12.4%)

④

② 81 (16.2%)

① 45 (9%)

③

103 (20.6%)

Vehicle Registration (Motor Car MCT 1903)
1ˢᵗ January 1904 (AF1) – February 1910 (AF500)

As all cars in Cornwall at 1 January 1904 had to be registered, this provided some indication of the number of vehicles already in the county. During the first week of registration fifty vehicles were registered and this increased to one hundred within a year. During that period 28,842 vehicles were registered in Great Britain. It was not until February 1910 that AF 500 was reached, issued to Major Hugh Bateman for both private use and in connection with his duties as Chief Constable of Cornwall. The car was a 16-20hp Wolseley Siddeley.

Fewer motorcycles, also starting with the registration AF1, were licensed. At this early period these were mainly pedal cycles with engines attached; more robust machines were to follow later. Of the motorcycles granted licenses in Cornwall during the period 1904 to February 1910 sixty-two were issued to addresses outside Cornwall by men serving with the Army at Bodmin Barracks, in the Navy or employed at Poldhu Wireless Station.[232]

An analysis of the first five hundred vehicles shows a heavy concentration in mid-Cornwall. Wealth was needed to own a car and here there would be industrialists, many of them with engineering interests, who possibly looked to develop car-production. This was certainly true of the Bickford and Bickford-Smith families of Trevarno: ten early cars went to members of this family, one licensed to the Bickford Motor Company in Camborne. Arthur Francis Bassett of Tehidy had no fewer than six of the first five hundred cars. Buying cars appeared to be almost an obsession with some gentry families who would have had the time as well as the money to indulge this interest. A breakdown of the owners of these first five hundred cars show:

- Private use 433, trade 122, public use 58. Total 614 (some vehicles registered for dual use).
- Eighty-two easily recognised from address and/or name as 'gentry'
- Fifteen doctors
- Eight clergy. Motor bikes were also popular with clergymen.
- Thirteen military (mainly officers at Bodmin Barracks)
- Seventeen steam vehicles (cars/lorries/tractors)

Of the forty-five vehicles shown as licensed in West Penwith, most were registered to addresses in Penzance. The exceptions were AF 276 and AF 423, licensed to Francis Oates of St Just for private use, and AF 348 owned by Dr Nesbitt, also of St Just. Col Cambourne Haweis Paynter of Boskenna, St Buryan, owned AF2, a steam-driven Serpolet. These were the only vehicles among the first five hundred with owners living closer to Land's End than Penzance. Despite this in an advertisement of 1912 the Land's End Hotel offered garage facilities in addition to stabling and a bicycle house. They represented both the Automobile Club of Great Britain and Ireland and the Motoring Union.

---

[232] CRO: CC3/13/1/1 to CC3/13/1/23 Registration records 1904 to 1920

Four cars among the forty-five were licensed to John Theodore Taylor who was trading as Taylor's Garage. These included two Darracq taxicabs, AF443 and AF480, purchased for the firm in 1909. The names Bazeley and Bolitho figure prominently in both early car- and motorcycle-registrations.

Mathias Dunn from Newlyn purchased a motorcycle in 1911 and a 20 hp Ford car in the following year. In 1913 Col. Paynter transferred the AF2 registration from his steam car to a 20-25 hp Overland Laudaulette. Charles Simpson registered an 8 hp Bat and sidecar (AF 1692) in June 1916, using the sidecar to carry his painting equipment. The artist Geoffrey Garnier purchased a licence for a motor bike in September 1913 (AF 948) and acquired another, a 3½ hp Douglas (AF 1070) in 1915. His son, Peter Garnier, was a life long motoring enthusiast, eventually becoming editor of *Autocar* he spent several seasons in the BMC rally team. In the licences recorded up until the end of 1920 for West Penwith, no further recognisable names of artists were noted. Others believed to have used motor vehicles before that date may have hired them from local garages.

Licences to drive both cars and motorcycles had to be renewed annually and so, after the first year, present problems in calculating numbers of licence-holders accurately from existing records. In 1904, the first year of issue, licences to drive cars or motorcycles were granted to 261 people throughout the whole of Cornwall, about a third more than the number of vehicles licensed. Obviously more than one person drove some vehicles. In West Penwith twenty-nine licences to drive were granted for both cars and cycles in the first year of registration, only thirteen of these to persons who had licensed cars. Looking through the registration records it becomes obvious that a number of car-owners employed chauffeurs but did not drive themselves. Some licences granted in 1904 were not renewed in the following year, many of these because the holder had gone abroad. In some instances the entry read 'gone to America' (or South Africa or Mexico)—reminders that emigration from Cornwall was at a high level in the first decade of the twentieth century.[233]

With the outbreak of the First World War increasing numbers of vehicles were licensed for military purposes, around seventy of them in Cornwall. Initially these were licensed to the Secretary of State for War with no reference to their destination within the county but as the war progressed the vehicles were assigned to specific sites, including the Air Station at Newlyn. From 1915 comparatively large numbers of privately owned cars and motorbikes were registered by service personnel, many with out-of-county addresses but now based in Cornwall. Most of these registrations were transferred or cancelled later in the war years.

In the early years following the establishment of the Highways, Bridges and Main Roads Committee attention centred on establishing responsibility for the maintenance of roads and bridges, especially where these might be used by heavy steam-locomotives. Responsibility for the cost of the upkeep of bridges was a frequent topic of discussion at quarterly committee meetings. Another topic concerned wastrals, the verges at the side of roads on land owned by farmers. It had become the custom for the authorities to pay the farmers for allowing them to dump stone there to repair roads. While the committee were advised by counsel that landowners could not insist on being paid, the committee, probably wisely, decided to go on doing so as the farmers might otherwise dump manure on the plots. (In later years the wastrals would again become a subject for discussion when it became necessary to widen roads to accommodate motor-cars.) By the 1890s the appropriate authorities were laying drains and gas pipes, and erecting telegraph poles, all interfering with the use of roads. At intervals the possibility of purchasing steamrollers for road-use was discussed, but it was 1897 before a few district councils were allowed to use them on an experimental basis. The first reference to motor-cars came at a meeting held on 18 January 1901 when a letter was received from the Secretary of the Automobile Club as to a reasonable limit being placed on the speed of motor-cars: the Committee were of the opinion that it should not exceed 12 mph, and a letter was sent to the Club to this effect.[234] The Automobile Club had been formed in 1897 and in 1907 became the RAC.

From now on there are more frequent references to West Penwith. The committee for that area had carried out experiments in steamrolling their main roads and in October 1904 decided to continue doing so for another season. At this time West Penwith had twenty-four and a half miles of designated main road. Increasingly there are references to road-widening, tar-spraying and steamrolling, kerbs, footpaths and requests for warning posts for motorists at dangerous points, the last tending to be

---

[233] CRO: CC/3/13/1/24
[234] CRO: CC/1/5/4

declined. In 1907 West Penwith were still trying to get the road between Penzance and Land's End designated a main road. Alexandra Road in Penzance was mained in 1912.

The question of damage to roads by military traffic came up for discussion in 1915 and it was found that the War Office would make a substantial contribution to the cost of repairs. In addition, where the military authorities required work to be carried out the cost could be reclaimed. This eventually proved of benefit to Newlyn when the road towards Mousehole was widened and strengthened to take traffic to the Air Station on the shore below Penlee Quarry. Immediately after the war this improvement enabled a motor-bus service to be set up between Penzance and Mousehole. Prior to the First World War those wishing to travel to Penzance relied on horse-drawn wagonettes and the carrier's cart. The wagonettes ran between Mousehole, Newlyn and the cab-stand at the top of Morrab road, Penzance. The owners of these did not turn to the new-fangled motors: the road surface was unmetalled there and was mud in winter and deep ruts and dust in summer, not to mention the many loose stones. Although the Great Western Railway (GWR) and other motor-bus services had been operating in the area since 1903, the width and surface of the road between Newlyn Bridge and Mousehole was considered unsuitable for such vehicles. Then, with former military vehicles of sturdier construction available for purchase at reasonable cost, the situation changed.

The Hitchens Brothers of Newlyn became the first to run a motor-bus service to Mousehole. In

1920's advertisement for the first bus service between Mousehole and Penzance.

December 1919 they bought a Napier fitted with a box-like saloon body and, with George Hitchens at the wheel, began a regular service each Tuesday, Thursday and Saturday, between Mousehole, Newlyn and the First and Last Inn at Penzance. The vehicle, registered AF2381, was christened 'Porth Enys', the old name for Mousehole. The service catered not only for local people, visitors were also encouraged to ride on 'The Finest Coastal Drive in the County'. This service continued to run until the summer of 1920, when George Hitchens left to go on a boat-trip around the world.

In Mousehole Nicholas Harvey saw that Hitchens' motor-bus service had met a local need, so he bought an ex-War Department Crossley fitted with an open 'jersey' body with seating for fourteen passengers. He started operating on the same route and was soon joined by George Hitchens brother, John Matthew, who got the family's Napier bus out of store and recommenced operations between Mousehole and Penzance. Despite the competition offered by Cornwall Motor Transport who moved into the Duchy from Devon in 1925, the Hitchens and Harveys worked in harmony, extending their services, and continued in business until 1988.[235]

At the end of the nineteenth century the GWR, following the arrival of the main line at Penzance, had been investigating the addition of branch lines, notably to coastal towns. Several proposals were put up for consideration but in many areas, including Penzance to Land's End, the cost was prohibitive and instead four horse-carriages were provided run by private operators. A real advance came in 1903, when a road motor service was inaugurated by the GWR from Helston to the Lizard, commencing on 17 August 1903. Two 16hp Milnes Daimler vehicles were purchased, eventually registered as AF 36 and AF37. These had open bodies except for a canopy roof and proved so successful that a further twenty-five vehicles were purchased and other routes were quickly opened up.

---

[235] Grimley

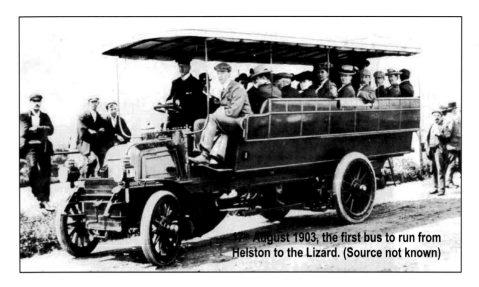

August 1903, the first bus to run from Helston to the Lizard. (Source not known)

The railway played a major part in the development of rural bus services in Cornwall, linking villages with the railways at an early date. From the first days of motoring in Cornwall, especially following the establishment of bus services by the GWR, private operators had seen the possibilities of bus tours as a tourist attraction. During the 1920s livery stables in Penzance were still running four-horse Jersey car tours and hiring out carriages to visitors. Their proprietors were able to compete and co-exist with garages offering motor-coach tours, both advertised in local guidebooks. Local garages also offered cars for private hire, with experienced drivers as required.

A feature of motor coach tours, such as those run by Trelawny Tours and the Western National Omnibus Company was 'Knowtoring—The Silent Guide Patented Service.' Passengers were provided with a booklet containing a map of the area and a description of each tour, commenting on points of interest along the route. Coaches were fitted with a device known as the *Scenaidicator* which displayed a number as each place of interest came into view, as the number changed a horn was sounded. Each number corresponded with a numbered section in the booklet, which provided some historical information and possibly an illustration. Day-tours would venture as far afield as Newquay; for the shorter morning or afternoon tours Land's End or St Ives were popular destinations. Mousehole and Newlyn rarely featured until the 1930s, when roads had improved. Tours were popular with local people as well as with visitors to the district. One Mousehole couple taking an evening mystery-tour found that their first destination, with a twenty-minute stop, was their own village. They went home and made a cup of tea.

Later, in the years following the 1939-45 war, long-distance tours of the West Country became popular. A seventy-two page, hardback illustrated booklet was presented to each passenger on a ten-day tour by Midland Red Motor Services in 1958. Tucked into the cover of each booklet is a card giving a day-to-day outline of the tour, while on the reverse is a list of passengers with their seat numbers. The card is headed 'Your fellow passengers on this cruise.' Coach tours, although they still continue, probably started to decline in number at about this point. Private ownership of cars was rising rapidly and overseas holidays were soon to come within reach of a growing section of the public.

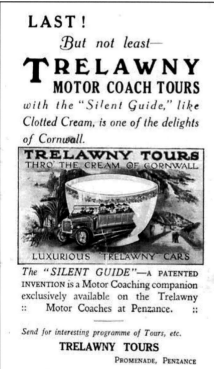

This advertisement for Trelawny Tours appeared on the back cover of the official guide to Penzance and Lands End for 1926

Reading accounts of the early days of motoring it becomes obvious that the possibility of travelling at speed was a great attraction. Despite legal limits the temptation to test out the capabilities of the engine on a straight stretch of road was hard to resist and many prosecutions for motoring offences were for speeding. It has to be said that the police seemed to rather enjoy setting traps for these early motorists which led to the formation of the AA—the Automobile Association—in 1905. The Automobile Club, later to become the RAC, had been formed in 1897. This organisation could be seen as elitist, a club for gentlemen with a common interest in motoring, but the AA was formed by militant motorists, initially with the aim of outwitting the police setting speed-traps. Here is the first secretary of the AA, Stenson Cooke, writing in the mid 1930s:

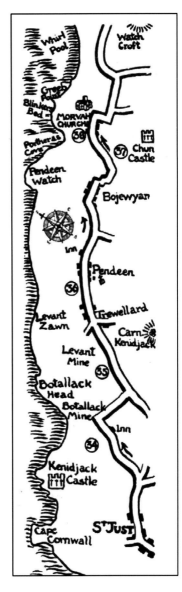

A measured furlong on a nice, straight piece of road, safe and tempting to the motorist. Two policemen in plain clothes, one at each end, with stop watches—hiding. A third in uniform, beyond the end of the measured distance... The scene was set. Law was lying in wait...enter the victim...

'Here he comes! Steady now, wait for it! Wait for it!'

Into the trap. Click went the watch, click, and wave of the handkerchief...Second timekeeper, a sergeant, on the ball now...Yes! He's covered the distance in less than...that's over twenty miles an hour. Caught!

Uniform, getting the signal, stalked into the middle of the road, with upheld hand. Stop![236]

The AA came up with the idea of enlisting youths from local cycling clubs to ride along stretches of road at weekends at places where traps were known to have been set, to warn motorists. This led to the membership scheme and the once familiar sight of AA patrolmen in their distinctive yellow and black uniforms. The famous salute to members was also, in their early days, a warning. The penalty for driving over the speed limit, or as it was described at the time 'furious driving,' was around ten shillings (50p) but at Penzance on 7 June 1909 Gordon Bert Ferne was fined £5 and costs for driving a motor vehicle to danger of the public, a considerable sum at that time.[237]

A page from Knowtouring a Western National coach tour guide, c1930

Another offence was driving without lights. In the early days of motoring these would have been oil lamps and some sympathy must be felt for Jasper Wilson, who in March 1903 pleaded guilty to driving a motor-car late at night without a light across Penzance promenade. The defendant said a gale was blowing and he could not keep the lights burning.[238] Inevitably there were more serious incidents: on 7 June 1909 at Mousehole the son of Mr Josiah F Trembath was knocked down by a motor-car at a dangerous corner and there were other accidents there.[239] On 30 June 1920 PC Botheras warned boys against riding on the back of motor lorries after Ivor Nicholls was injured.[240]

As the motoring age entered the 1920s, manufacture speeded up when the production line system was introduced. Ford production had come to Britain in 1911, and Morris Minor production began in 1928 with prices starting at £125. The year 1926 saw the first use of safety glass in windscreens, which was to become compulsory from 1937. Traffic signs had begun to put in an appearance. Single white lines were introduced as road dividers in 1927, and the same year saw the first automated traffic lights. Driving tests commenced on 1 June 1935 and today, little more than 100 years since the first car was seen in Cornwall, almost every seventeen-year-old in the county will be looking forward to taking lessons and owning their own car.

---

[236] Cooke
[237] CRO: JC/PENW/2
[238] *Royal Cornwall Gazette*
[239] CRO: DC/PEN 286, 202
[240] CRO: SR/PAU/2/7

Bibliography

Archives and interviews

AC: interview with Anne Crockett 31 May 2004

BP: interview with Church Elder, Billy Perkin, 20 December 2006

CBCO archive: CBCO archive, Friends House Library

CCC: **Cornish Congregational Church records,** CRO X682

Chirgwin Archive: Papers of R Chirgwin & Son Ltd, MOR/CHl, Morrab Library

Clifford Harry's manuscript notes in possession of Carlene Harry

CRO: Cornwall Record Office

Goldsithney Logbooks: Cornwall Record Office SR/PERU/1-4 (1871-1969)

Index: Index CC Committees 26, Cornwall Record Office, Truro

JPV: J Patrick Vaughan, interviews and e-mails 2004-07

NFS A: National Farm Survey, TNA MAF 32/451/188/3 (dated 15 January 1942)

NFS T: National Farm Survey, TNA MAF 32/411/2/92 (dated 7 August 1942)

Noall: C Noall, Zion Congregationalist Church at St Ives (MS at the Cornish Methodist Historical Association Library, Cornwall Centre, Redruth)

PB: interview with Pip Benveniste (née Walker) 22 November 2006, and subsequent e-mails

SEG: Sue Griffin, née Watson: interviews and e-mails

Shears Archive (private)

Tate Archive GB

WH: William Hetherington, PPU Archivist, private communications

Wheal Betsy Archive (private)

Zennor WI: Zennor WI, 'The Changing Farm 1900-1980', unpublished MS, Cornwall County Record Office, WI/ZEN/6/2

Zennor WI Diary: 'Zennor Women's Institute Millennium Diary 2000', unpublished, Cornwall County Record Office, WIZEN

Censuses

Parish Registers

Kelly's Directories

Newspapers and magazines

The Architect and Building News, 1944

The Builders Journal and Architectural Record, 1896

Cornishman: the *Cornishman* (newspaper), (1878-)

Cornish Telegraph: the *Cornish Telegraph* (newspaper) (1851-1915)

Evening Tidings: this paper was the daily edition of the *Cornish Telegraph* (see above).

The Guardian

Royal Cornwall Gazette

The Studio, 1895-8

Printed Books, Articles and Websites

Ancestry.com: http://ancestry.com/

Anderson & Koval: Organize Anderson and A Koval, *James McNeill Whistler: Beyond the Myth* (London, 1994)

Anon: Anonymous, *Meeting House and Burial Ground of the Religious Society of Friends at Marazion* (privately published, 1999)

Architects' Journal 1940: 'Senior girls' school, Penzance; Designed by A. Geoffrey Bazeley, G. H. Ineson', *Architects' Journal* 1940 Apr. 18, p. 412. Cited in the RIBA Catalogue at http://195.171.22.30/uhtbin/cgisirsi.exe/rX9CQTLyVX/0/0/49

Ball: Richard Ball, *Congregationalism in Cornwall*, (London, 1956)

Bender: B Bender, S Hamilton and C Tilley, 'Leskernick; Stone Worlds; Alternative Narratives; Nested Landscapes', *Proceedings of the Prehistoric Society* 63 (1997): 147-78

Benton: Tim and Charlotte Benton with Dennis Sharpe, *Form and Function: A Source Book for the History of Architecture and Design 1890-1939* (London, 2000)

Billingham: Peter Billingham, *Theatres of Conscience 1939-45: a Study of Four Touring British Community Theatres* (London, 2002)

Borlase: W Borlase, *Observations of the Antiquities, Historical and Monumental, of the County of Cornwall,* (Oxford 1754)

Brittain: Vera Brittain, *Thrice a Stranger* (London, 1938)

Brown CG: Callum G Brown, *Religion and Society in the Twentieth Century Britain* (Harlow, 2006)

Brown HM: H. Miles Brown, *A Century for Cornwall* (Truro, 1977)

Bullen: LJ Bullen. *Mining in Cornwall Vol. 3 Penwith and South Kerrier*, (Stroud, 2005)

Buller: Rev J Buller, *St Just in Penwith: a Statistical Account*, (1842, reprinted Truro, 1983)

Cahill: NJ Cahill and the Cornish Archeological Unit, *St Just*, (Cornwall County Council, 2002)

Calloway: Stephen Calloway (ed), *The Elements of Style* (London, 1996)

Camden: W Camden, *Britannia,*(London 1586)

Carew: R Carew, *The Survey of Cornwall* (London 1602)

C.A.S: Cornwall Archaeological Society at www.cornisharchaeology.org.uk (2007)

CB: *The Community Broadsheet*

CBCO Analysis: CBCO Analysis of Appellate Tribunals, *CBCO Bulletin*, vol organize, Organize 1940 (no pagination)

Chesher: Veronica Chesher (ed) *Newlyn Life, 1870-1914 : the Village that Inspired the Artists* (Penwith Local History Group, 2003) (out of print)

Cooke: Stenson Cooke *This Motoring—Being the Romantic Story of the Automobile Association**Error! Bookmark not defined.** (London, 1937)

Corin: J Corin, *Levant: A Champion Cornish Mine*, (Camborne, 1992)

Cornish Mining World Heritage: web pages (St Just area) at http://www.cornish-mining.org.uk/sites/stjust.htm

Courtney: JS Courtney, 'Statistical remarks on St Just in Penwith,' *Annual Report of the RCPS* (1841) (RCPS = Royal Cornwall Polytechnic Society)

Dellar: Pamela Dellar, ed *Plays Without Theatres—Recollections of the Compass Players Travelling Theatre 1944-1952* (Beverley, 1989)

De Vey: George and Simon De Vey, *Anderton and Rowland*, (research by Stephen Smith, booklet from *Cornishman*, 21 June 1900

Dempsey: Amy Dempsey, *Styles, Schools and Movements* (London, 2002)

Densham: Ian Densham, 'Sherwood, Selina and Salubrious Place' (paper delivered to the Congregational Studies Conference, 1994; reprinted as a booklet, nd)

Drury: Michael Drury, *Wandering Architects* (Stamford, 2000)

Easton: David Easton, The Closure of Methodist Chapels since 1932 (Unpublished MA Thesis, University of Exeter, 2002)

Faulkner: T Ewen Faulkner, 'Tribunal Decisions Considered' *CBCO Bulletin*, vol ii, April 1942: 6-7

Gray: AS Gray, *Edwardian Architecture* (London, 1988)

Green: Iris M Green, *Posing the Model: a Study of Students of Stanhope Forbes' Newlyn School of Painting 1899-1941* (Penzance, 2002)

Griffiths: Richard Griffiths, 'A Note on Mosley, the 'Jewish War' and Conscientious Objection' *Journal of Contemporary History*, Vol 40/4 (October 2005), pp. 675-688; précis at http://www.history.ac.uk/ihr/Resources/Books/00220094.html

Grimley: Roger Grimley *The Mouzel Bus: the Story of Motor Buses from Mousehole and Newlyn* (Bigbury, 1998)

Guthrie: A Guthrie, *Cornwall in the Age of Steam*, (Padstow, 1994)

Hamilton Jenkin (b): AK Hamilton Jenkin, *Mines and Miners of Cornwall*, (Truro 1961)

Hatje: Gerd Hatje (Ed), *Encyclopaedia of Modern Architecture* (London, 1963)

Heald: Henrietta Heald (ed), *Chronicle of Britain: incorporating a Chronicle of Ireland* (Farnborough, 1992)

Hencken: H O'Neill Hencken, *The Archaeology of Cornwall and Scilly* (London 1932)

Hough: Richard Hough (ed) *Motor-Car Lover's Companion* (London, 1965)

Hudson: K Hudson, 'Industrial Archaeology in the South-West', *Cornish Archaeology* 3 (1964) 80-83

Hughes: Jennifer Hughes (co-ordinator), A century of shops in St. Just-in-Penwith (St. Just Women's Institute, 2000)

Ince: Catherine Ince (selected and edited by), *Life in Cornwall 1939-1942 extracts from the* West Briton *newspaper* (Truro, 2000)

Ineson: GH Ineson, *Community Journey* (The Catholic Book Club, [1956])

Isaac: Peter Isaac, *A History of Evangelical Christianity in Cornwall* (Penzance, 1999)

Jekyll: Gertrude Jekyll, 'How the house was built', reprinted from *Home and Garden* (1900), in *Antique Collectors Club* (1982): 22-35

Jenkin (1921): AK Hamilton Jenkin, *The Cornish Miner: An Account of His Life Above and Under Ground From Early Times*, (London, 1927)

Johns: C Johns, 'An Iron Age Sword and Mirror Cist Burial from Bryher, Isles of Scilly', *Cornish Archaeology* Vol. 41-42 (2002-2003): 1-79

Langworthy: D Langworthy, *The Balmaidens & Children on the Dressing Floors of Levant Mine* (nd)

Lea: Frank Lea, *The Life of John Middleton Murry* (London, 1959)

Leeds: ET Leeds, 'Excavations at Chun Castle, Penwith', *Archaeology* 76 (1926-27) 205

Leland: J Leland, *The Itinerary* (Oxford 3rd edn. 1770)

Levy: N Levy, *The Foundations of the South African Cheap Labour System*, (London, 1982)

Lewis: AL Lewis, 'Cornish Quoits and French Dolmens – a comparison', *Journal of the RIC* Vol.xviii (1910): 409-412

Livingstone & Parry: Karen Livingstone & Linda Parry, *International Arts and Crafts* (London [Organize&A], 2005)

Lomax (a): Pamela Lomax, *The Long Engagement* (Newlyn, 2002)

Lomax (b): Pamela Lomax, *The Golden Dream* (Sansom, 2004)

Makin: John L Makin, 'Pacifist Farming Communities in Lincolnshire in World War Two' (now published East Midland Historian, Vol 14, 2004, pp 49-63)

Mann: Arthur and Nora Mann, 'Notes for their Talks', *Cornwall Association of Local Historians Journal,* Spring 2002

Marsden: (1919): JG Marsden, 'Note on flint and other stone implements from south west Penwith', *Journal of the RIC,* Vol.20 (1919) 483-496

    (1921): JG Marsden, 'Flint Implements of Le Moustier Type from Camborne', *Journal of the RIC,* Vol.21 (1921) 48-55

    (1922): JG Marsden, 'Some unrecorded Prehistoric Sites in West Penwith', *Journal of the RIC,* Vol.22 (1922) 169-174

Mayers: L Mayers, *Balmaidens*, (Penzance, 2004)

Monthly Return of Sea Fisheries Statistics: Marine and Fisheries Agency, Monthly Return of Sea

Fisheries Statistics for England, Wales, Scotland and Northern Ireland (*Provisional*) (May 2007) http://www.mfa.gov.uk/statistics/documents/monthlyseafishstats.pdf

Murry: John Middleton Murry, *Community Farm* (Country Book Club, London: 1953)

Muthesius: Hermann, 'The Meaning of Arts and Crafts 1907', Benton, Tim and Charlotte Benton with Dennis Sharpe, *Form and Function: A Source Book for the History of Architecture and Design 1890-1939* (London, 2000)

Nankervis: Jean Nankervis, *The Traditional Farm: Wicca, Zennor, St Ives, Cornwall* (Zennor, 1989)

Nauright: J Nauright, 'Cornish Miners and the Witwatersrand Gold Mines in South Africa, 1890-1904', *Cornish History* 2001

Newton: William G Newton, *FABS: An Outline History* (London, 1930)

Noall (1970): C Noall, *The Mine Below the Sea*, (Truro, 1970)

Payton: P Payton, *The Cornish Overseas*, (revised edn, Fowey, 2005)

Penhale: Jack Penhale, *The Mine Under the Sea*, (Falmouth, 1962)

Penhaul: Chunky Penhaul, Old Codgers, *The Mermaid's Echo, [the Zennor Parish Magazine]*, 31 (Easter 2006):25-7

Perry: R Perry, 'Cornwall's Mining Collapse Revisited', *Cornish History* 2001

Peters: Caradoc Peters, *The Archaeology of Cornwall,* (Fowey 2005)

Pool: PAS Pool, *History of the Town and Borough of Penzance* (Pz, 1974)

PPU COB: Peace Pledge Union, Conscientious Objection in Britain during the Second World War at http://www.ppu.org.uk/learn/infodocs/cos/st_co_wwtwo.html

PPU COP: Peace Pledge Union, CO Project, http://www.ppu.org.uk/coproject/guide.html

Rigby: A Rigby, 'Pacifist communities in Britain in the Second World War', *Peace & Change,* 15(2), April 1990

Rogers: W Rogers, 'A Kitchen Midden on Godrevy Towans', *Journal of the RIC* ,Vol xviii (1909) 238-240

Rose-Troup: Frances Rose-Troup, *The Western Rebellion of 1549* (London, 1913)

Scott: ORG Baillie Scott, 'The Decoration of the Suburban House', *The Studio* No 25, 1895

Smith: Christopher Smith, *150 years of Catholicism in Penzance* (Penzance, 1994)

Stone: J Harris Stone, *England's Riviera,* (London 1912)

Stray: C Stray, 'The Pen is Mightier Than the Spade; archaeology and education in Nineteenth Century England', *Pharos* Vol.10 (2002): 123-134

Symons: Alison Symons, *Tremedda Days*, (Tabb House, 1992)

Tarrant: Michael Tarrant. *Cornwall's Lighthouse Heritage* (Truro, 2000)

Thomas: Charles Thomas, *Phillack Church*, (Hayle, 1960)

Trounson: JH Trounson, *The Cornish Mineral Industry*, (Exeter, 1989)

Utopia: Utopia Britannica – British Utopian Experiments 1325-1945, at http://www.utopia-britannica.org.uk/pages/whiteway.htm

Vision of Britain: A Vision of Britain Through Time (Historical GIS Project) www.visionofbritain.org.uk

Weeks: Ann Weeks *A Family Concern : S. Hicks and Son Ltd, 1876-1976* (Truro 1976)

Yorke: Trevor Yorke, *The Edwardian House Explained* (Newbury, 2006)

INDEX

117